Syncopated Rhythms

by

Paul Rabinowitz

Finishing Line Press
Georgetown, Kentucky

Syncopated Rhythms

Copyright © 2025 by Paul Rabinowitz
ISBN 979-8-89990-287-1 First Edition
All rights reserved under International and Pan-American Copyright Conventions. No part of this book may be reproduced in any manner whatsoever without written permission from the publisher, except in the case of brief quotations embodied in critical articles and reviews.

ACKNOWLEDGMENTS

I would like to thank these magazines, journals and presses for giving homes to versions of the stories found in this book during the past few years: "The Studio": *Barely South Review*; "Little Death": *Wrath-Bearing Tree*; "Unknown Author": *The Metaworker*; "Moriah Heights": *Epoque Magazine*; "Syncopated Rhythms": *Grey Sparrow*; "Post-It Note": *La Piccioletta Barca*; "Netflix Thriller": *Sonora Review*; "On The Eighth Day": *October Hill Magazine*; "Diamond Life Master": *La Piccioletta Barca*; "Little Gem Magnolia": *The Metaworker Literary Journal*; "The Ending": *Stoneboat Literary Journal*; "Portrait of Unknown Woman: Coney Island": *La Piccioletta Barca*.

I would also like to thank Michelle Ortega, E Catanese and Tamar Jacobs for their editing, suggestions and support.

Publisher: Leah Huete de Maines
Editor: Christen Kincaid
Cover Art: Anna Hershinow
Author Photo: Megan Rabinowitz
Cover Design: Elizabeth Maines McCleavy

Order online: www.finishinglinepress.com
also available on amazon.com

Author inquiries and mail orders:
Finishing Line Press
PO Box 1626
Georgetown, Kentucky 40324
USA

Contents

Moriah Heights 1

Little Gem Magnolia 21

Portrait of Unknown Woman: Coney Island 27

Netflix Thriller 35

Big Game 36

The Other Side of the Moon 52

The Studio 85

Little Death 88

Unknown Author 90

Syncopated Rhythms 92

On The Eighth Day 93

Diamond Life Master 110

The Ending 121

Syncopation is a disturbance of the regular flow of rhythm, a placement of rhythmic stresses or accents where they wouldn't normally occur.

Moriah Heights

A broken clothesline leans
against its shadow

nothing to hang memories
on

through the stillness of the desert landscape
I meander

fragrance of creosote bush
underfoot

dry winds blow clockwise
shifting transverse ridges of sand

In the distance a prickly pear cactus
tempts the coyote

despite needles
the coyote consumes its fruit

spreading seeds

every thing
transient

even the shadows

I stuff my backpack with the basic essentials, orient my body toward the west and head out into the cooling desert. Barren hills unfold in abstract patterns against the fading orange and yellow light. During the past year I've learned much since I left my suburban New York home. I gave up most of the possessions I amassed in my 55 years on the planet.

I've evolved and transformed parts of myself to adapt in my new environment. I no longer fear the desert. I trust the land and what it offers. I accept everything now and better understand its purpose. I've learned to let things go and see where they fall.

I squint my eyes as the last rays of the setting sun pull back. The fragrance of sagebrush smells sweet. Next to a prickly pear cactus a pile of stones mark the point where I enter the river bed and the path begins. Last month after two days of torrential rains, this serene spot had turned into a violent river. Flash flooding had occurred when the banks could not hold the volume of water. Dried creeks became raging rivers. A child playing in his backyard was swept away. They searched every inch of the land but could not find him. His parents own a condo at Moriah Heights. He was their only child.

As I approach my night time perch, a faint cluster of stars appears in the darkening sky.

"Once the stars appear you'll want to stay on that rock outcropping all night," Mike had said.

Mike was my boss and the person who hired me. A native to the area and head sales manager at Moriah Heights.

"Be careful out there. The river bed can be tricky at night."

"I'll be fine."

He leaned in close and put his hand on my shoulder.

"What kind of name is Eli?"

"It's from the Bible," I said.

"It's got some kind of meaning?"

"Elevated one."

He squeezed my shoulder with his fingers.

"Nice. Well. Listen, the desert plays tricks on us. No trees to orient direction. You've got water, right?"

"Right."

"And remember, I'll need you at work at 6:30. Gotta get your rounds done before it gets too hot. Don't want you to dehydrate and pass out."

Mike was tall with a tanned face and sharp features. He wore a cowboy hat with a huge turquoise stone attached to a braided string. He always had a pouch attached to his belt. Mike reminded me of one of those cowboys from the old rodeo posters. He was Navajo. I couldn't see it, but then again, of course, there are plenty of things we can't see. Mike was stoic. At times he was elusive or maybe just stoned. But I learned to trust him. He mentored me in the ways of the land and reminded me why folks come out here to live.

"We got a lot of good paying residents here and their condos need to be attended to. They come here to enjoy the surroundings. Our job is to provide the best service to let them do that."

My mind wandered and lingered on the grieving parents.

"You with me, Eli?"

"Yeah, sorry. I'm here."

"Respond to their needs quickly and always with a smile."

I was soon thrown into all kinds of situations. From removing half-eaten poodles to extracting bats living in people's homes.

"Trap 'em one by one with cardboard boxes," Mike had said. "If one's rabid and you get bitten you're a dead man walking."

He knew everything about his surroundings but not much else. He was a survivor. I envied that. Once in a while I'd test him and ask about world news or the declining stock market. He moved his head to the side and squinted his eyes.

"It'll change."

Even when I told him something uplifting, he'd reply the same way.

Along the sides of the path a mariposa lily bloomed in spite of the harsh climate. Mike had said that in the fall the flowers shed their seeds and germinate right before the winter rains come. Several years will pass before a bulb reaches maturity and produces a flower.

"Because they're buried deep in the earth, they can survive wildfires. They take advantage of the nutrient-rich soil and lack of competition from other plants so the bulbs produce greater numbers of flowers than in average years."

"We should all have patience like the mariposa," I said.

"If you're ever lost and have no food, you unearth their bulbs and eat them. Raw is ok, but I suggest making a fire and roasting 'em."

I climb to the top of the rock and set down my backpack. The rocky landscape spills out before me as the sky darkens. Tonight there is a new moon, so the night sky will be at its blackest. The best time of the month to view what's out there. In the distance yip-howls of a male and female coyote pierce the night sky.

"Without a canopy of trees their harmonies swirl. It's a chaotic mix of sound, I don't know how else to describe it," Mike had said. "This confuses their predators to think they are surrounded by a pack of hundreds. It's an auditory illusion known as the 'beau geste' effect, caused by a variety of sounds produced by a male and female coyote and gets distorted as it passes through the barren land."

During my evening walks my thoughts wandered in non-linear ways. Sometimes I wondered if a traveler like me ever passed through here before, someone from outside. Maybe they were also trying to figure out their life. I was here for a purpose. Not everyone leaves everything they strived for in their lives to one day just up and go. Mike liked to say we are all bound by some kind of fate. I wasn't sure I agreed but listened to his rationale. If I was to leave my past world behind and maybe find my son, I knew I had to listen closely to what he had to say. He understood this world I had come to live in. He understood the moon and cycles and the creatures that called this harsh land its home. He didn't read books to get his knowledge. He walked the land and lived on it, was part of it.

Are we bound by fate?

Upon reaching the top of the outcropping, I lay on my back and look up at the infinite sky. The stars pulsate as if they are signaling something. I cover my ears with the palms of my hands and watch for a sign.

During the first few weeks at my new desert community, I'd received a stream of texts from friends back home. They didn't let up for a long time.

"How was your awakening today?" they'd ask. "You find God?"

They'd predicted I wouldn't last more than a year. It was a matter of time before I'd come running back to the land of milk and honey.

"How's the autumn colors…on the one tree?"

They made fun of the odd names of the gated communities; Bethel Hills, Canaan Vista and of course, Moriah Heights.

"Watch out for the Red Sea; it can part at any moment, right?"

I landed a job pretty quickly.

"Pretty basic work for an MIT graduate," they said.

Eventually I grew tired of their arrogance and sarcasm and stopped texting them back. I had my job and a rent-free cottage. It was all I needed. With a master's degree in Mechanical Engineering I was able to figure things out pretty quickly.

"You're in charge of all the maintenance at our wonderful gated community," Mike said. "The infrastructure at Moriah Heights is your responsibility."

"Got it."

"I'll get the folks to buy in," he said, extending his hand. "You keep it running."

After 25 years behind the computer screen and endless meetings with clients, menial tasks and manual labor suited me just fine.

"Every morning you'll pick up the garbage in the communal areas and sweep away the encroaching sand."

My new job had allowed me the space I needed to clear my head. I even bought myself an easel and tried my hand at painting.

Leaving behind what I had, or what I lacked, was not a hard decision. My wife and I were no longer speaking to each other. My job stressed me out to the point I started drinking to self-medicate. I hated myself and my world, and the only thing that kept me grounded was my son, Zach. Once he left, or disappeared, I had no reason to stay.

"He must be using drugs," my wife said, staring into space.

"I don't think so, darling. We would have seen signs."

"Maybe he met someone or was abducted by some white supremacist group."

These questions had gone on endlessly.

"You're his father and you don't give a shit."

"I do."

"So do something. Call the police."

I cared more about Zach than anything else in my life. The fact she couldn't see that is what put me over the edge.

"How could an eighteen-year-old boy just get up and go without telling you where?"

Our friends hadn't been able to comprehend it. They were educated and rational people. We all moved to New York City after college. What was once cool and gritty now became a place they did not want for their children.

"The place has turned into a dangerous shithole. Not what it used to be when we lived there? I don't want my kids to be exposed to it."

Like a disease.

Most of our friends' kids went to school with Zach. The school was considered one of the most competitive private schools in the country.

"The Jettisons are sending Tommy there," my wife said.

"He'll be sheltered."

"Yeah, sheltered among the right people."

Everything was for Zach so arguing with her was futile. As our only child she had him always in her rearview mirror. He was destined to repeat her father's success as a top neurosurgeon. He was just a few days away from beginning the dream of every Westchester parent. Our friends termed it the *great trek*. One studies to seek wealth. No time to waste, so at 18 their children had set their goals. If it wasn't law school, med school or an MBA in finance, nothing mattered. They wanted their children's academic path to ensure greater wealth than they had amassed. The American dream. Alive and well and flourishing in Westchester thanks to my friends.

The great trek.

"He's destined to be a brain surgeon," she said.

I looked up from an article I was reading about the rapid pace of advancement with DNA sampling.

"We don't know."

"I'm his mother," she said "I know."

Later I would regret not trying to find words to talk to her about this rigid fixation, this desire for our son to find and walk the great trek without first finding himself. My God, how I regretted it.

A day before his departure for college the walls came tumbling down. His best friend's parents put together a BBQ and swim party for his class. A going away party and possibly the last time they'd see each other until Thanksgiving or Christmas break. Some were going to Stanford and already had plans to stay with family for the holidays in Marin County. Their *great trek* would begin in Silicon Valley. The goal was to land an internship at a tech firm to get their foot in the door. We planned with Zach that he'd come home right after the party. He'd help us seal up the boxes and carry them out to our SUV.

"How about you pick up sushi on the way home," I'd said.

"Sounds like a plan, Dad."

We used to love our sushi dinners together on Friday nights. Just the three of us chatting about everything from the books we were reading or films we'd seen. There was plenty of conversation to go around as we shared our sushi and dunked our rolls into the soy sauce. We never wanted those evenings to end. This was before my wife developed her singular focus on what came next for him, his great trek toward neurosurgery. After that the frequency of our sushi dinners slowed down.

"It'll be really hard when he goes to college," she said one night as she laid in bed.

I put down my book and rolled over to comfort her. Tears rolled down her cheek and pooled on her pillow.

"It'll be OK," I said, touching her shoulder. "We'll have more time together to do things. You'll see."

She rolled away and disconnected. My hand dropped.

"Can you turn off your light, please. I'm done."

Done.

As I wrapped and taped the last box and slid it to the side of the room for Zach, I heard my phone go off. There was a long thread of texts from Zach.

The last one read, "I'm not in control of myself. My thoughts are not in sync with my body."

I was uneasy and didn't know what to say or do.

"Hey Zach, I'll call you now."

There was no answer.

"Give me a call as soon as you get this message," I texted.

I saw the three dots and felt relief at this evidence of his presence on the other end.

"I have this recurring dream," he texted. "I'm on a ladder, painting a ceiling. Then a blinding light enters the room through a crack in the roof. I can't see the whole picture. It's like this great, bright light coming out of the sky."

For some reason my thoughts jumped to our walks in the woods together when he was about six years old. He'd had so many questions.

"Where does color come from?"

"I'm not exactly sure but I'll look it up when we get home."

"Also, where does light come from? And do magnetic fields produce sparks? Why does the earth revolve a certain way around the sun?"

He never stopped. More and more of my days were spent researching to find a logical answer for a six-year-old. I was so proud of my son's mind, or his hunger to understand the world.

"Dad is it true there's a person out there that does all this?"

I'd tried to answer in ways that would make sense to him. He'd wanted truths and I could only hand him more mysteries.

"Is there like a switch?"

"You'll figure it all out one day."

"How d'you know, dad?"

"I don't know for a fact, but I have a feeling."

What else could I say?

By the time he'd entered high school he started to care less about sports and hanging out with his friends. He would spend hours on the Internet searching information about light, the sun and the interior of the Sistine Chapel. My wife thought it highly unusual for a teenage suburban kid to give up his social life for this.

"It'll pass," I assured her.

Although somehow I believed it would not. I looked back down at my phone as a new text came in.

"I'll text you tomorrow once I have this all figured out."

I had a strange feeling in my stomach that the text would never come.

After Zach disappeared, I had to make a decision. Either I hire an investigator to look for him, or I sit tight, and let this new change happen. I believed in my heart that something would shift and he would see something that might solve his internal dilemma. I chose to wait. I myself had conviction that all things come if given the right amount of space and patience. The wealthy 'burbs of Westchester County didn't afford him either. I had my own thoughts as to where he might end up or when that call would come.

"I know we could have done something to prevent this," my wife said, stone-faced, and I heard what she really meant: she knew I could have done something to prevent this, *should have* done something to prevent this.

"We did the best we could," I said, speaking as much to myself as to my wife.

After his disappearance, our lives began to unravel. I began to have stomach flare-ups that would last for days. When I came home from work she'd be sitting there with a gin and tonic in one hand and her cell phone in the other.

"Did you speak to him about this?"

She was actually closer to the truth than she knew, but we couldn't discuss it.

"No dear. I just think we should give him time."

"I hate you," she said and refilled her glass with gin.

Things were changing shape irrevocably, though maybe this had begun long before Zach disappeared.

At work everyone knew what had happened and no one agreed with my decision. Some of them knew Zach and they thought I did the most unparental thing one could do.

"An animal would never do that."

I shrugged it off. They were helicopter parents who didn't trust themselves so how could one expect them to trust their own children. I believe we haven't fully evolved yet. The more we accept this, the greater our understanding of our needs and ability to survive.

"Survival is the only way," I said. "Zach is figuring out something now for his future survival."

We protected him like a seed in a greenhouse for too many years. He was a naive kid. No animal would do that to their offspring. If I didn't let go now he would be stunted. At some point he would have no idea how to get through the turbulence of life. I feared he had no way to swallow the bitter pill. That was our fundamental difference.

So on a sunny spring day, I poured myself a gin and tonic and sat down next to my wife.

"Looks like you'll let the garden grow wild this year?"

I handed my boss my resignation letter. I also met with our family attorney.

"We'll be fine, or I should say you'll be fine. You'll get monthly checks and can stay in the house for as long as you want. If you ever want to sell, he'll be there to help you. You keep everything from the sale so there's nothing to argue over."

She turned her head in my direction and sipped her drink.

"I love Zach more than anything. That's why I didn't go after him. I want to hear his voice and walk with him again. I know it might be a while, but something in my gut tells me he's alright and recalibrating. I'll let you know when I see him. I'm sure he would have found what he was looking for. My hope is it will happen soon."

I glanced over at her blank stare.

"You know it all, don't you."

I took a deep breath.

"One thing I am sure about, he is never coming back here."

"Don't forget to charge the Tesla, Honey. Don't want you to get stuck in the middle of nowhere."

And like that I was gone.

I had this weird feeling the farther west I drove, the closer I'd be to him. The sunsets became more vivid as the trees gave way to shrub brush, then open land and eventually desert. I thought about the setting of the stories in the Bible. The characters were always wandering about in barren lands like these. Whether it was a verdant oasis or near wells, the writers were also on a search. Their great trek was full of rich stories with metaphors and allegories. Stories of real people grappling with the same questions we deal with today. One thing was for certain, my Tesla's charge was low.

"Heard you resigned?" my friend from the lab texted. "You heading out to find him?"

"No."

My colleagues are engineers and scientists. Their experiments yield concrete and tangible results. They understand logic. Anything else is incomprehensible.

It took me a few months to acclimate to living in the desert. The light and heat was unbearable when the sun was high but at night the land cooled down. I grew to love the yip-howl of the coyotes. It was a great sacrifice to be out here but felt right. I had come to realize over the past few years that I needed to change. I had to reset my compass and set my priorities right. If not I'd die a lonely death surrounded by people who thought they knew me. That frightened me. On that spring day when I backed out of the garage of my Westchester house, I knew it was the last time I'd ever see it. I'd start to focus on my day to day existence. I wanted to get in touch with myself and finally, get to know myself. I wanted to know what it was that I feared and what I truly loved. There was also a chance I might never see Zach again. I thought about this in my walks in the beautiful sunsets. The hours of solitude. I was at peace with it but hoped there was a reason for all of it.

I'd remembered peeking into his room before he left for his friend's going away party.

"Zach?"

He'd appeared to be almost in a trance. He was on the Internet looking at photos of the Sistine Chapel.

"What d'you know about this," he said.

He didn't move his eyes from the computer screen.

"I'm a bit confused these days, Dad."

"About what?"

"Do we have power over our own lives?"

I sat down on his bed.

"Like let's say I want to go against everything that was planned out for me. Just go."

"Just go?"

He turned his chair around and leaned in close to me.

"Do we have any control over ourselves?" he whispered. "Any power to move in our own direction? If we become subservient to fate will the human race end up in despair? What if we resist it all?"

These days while on my evening desert meanders, I think about the same things. I don't want to fade away like dust and die a lonely man in a world of familiar people. Like him, I had to move on and continue to live, even if it meant giving up everything I had and starting from the beginning.

When I got home from my star gazing, I'd sit down on my computer until late into the night and check if there was any sign on Zach's social media sites. His pages were set up, but he deleted his headshots.

One day Mike and I went out for beers. He advised me to stop thinking about him and unfollow him.

"Don't get sucked into your curiosity. You'll become an obsessed man."

"I already am. How do I unfollow my own son? Tell me this."

He bought me a beer and told me the story of his Navajo grandfather.

"He carried a little pouch with him whenever he went out. Told me it was to collect memories 'cause they don't last. We forget and they fade."

"He plucked at leaves from the chaparral and steeped it for tea. It tasted like shit but out of respect we drank it."

"You'll remember that," his grandfather said.

"We sure did."

He went on to tell me about his wife's battle with cancer. She was his high school sweetheart. They got married at 21 and she was diagnosed with a rare cancer a few years later.

"After she passed I was devastated. I was like this walking zombie. My grandfather said to forget her. Put her out of your memory."

"That's tough."

"She was the only girl I ever had so it was hard, but my grandfather had this wisdom of years. We all respected him so I figured it was worth trying."

"When you can no longer remember what she looked like you will get a sign," his grandfather said. "Then you can search for her spirit."

Mike leaned forward. I could feel his breath.

"Some said he was crazy but I believed in him. There's lots of magic around here."

I was beginning to understand.

"Get off of his Facebook page," Mike said. "Stop searching."

He signaled to the bartender for the check.

"Supposed to be a great sunset tonight," he said. "Let's take a look."

He put his arm around me and sang a few verses of an old Eagles song. I sang with him.

"Strange concept," I said.

"The sunset?"

I waited before answering him.

"To forget everything."

During the next few days I'd tried everything to block out memories. If my thoughts wandered back to Westchester, or to Zach, I'd shut my eyes and remember the lyrics to the Eagles song. I kept busy with my handyman work. It helped to get my mind off Zach and everything in my past. One day I got a call from my attorney in New York about our investments. My wife needed more money for new medications. Our insurance wasn't covering them so I made some calls. I laid down on my couch and thought about the mess I left back home.

"When you start to drift back, go out and find the creosote bush," Mike said. "Rub the leaves and inhale. It extracts moisture from parched soil through its root system so the leaves smell like rain. They're hearty bastards and can withstand high temperatures and dehydration. Put some leaves in your pouch. They cure all kinds of ailments. My grandfather called the bush the anointed one."

After a few weeks I actually started to forget. I had my work during the morning and afternoon, the sunsets in the evening and star gazing on my perch at night. Folks in the complex started warming to me. I stayed off all social media and only used the Internet to learn more about the desert. I even started to read the Old Testament as Mike hounded me every day about my name and the meaning. I told him about the namesake of the complex where we lived. He was intrigued about the story of Abraham and his son.

"I could never kill my son."

"It's just a metaphor," I said. "He was being tested."

"For what?"

I thought of my life. How all of it felt like a test.

I spot a coyote in the distance tearing at a cactus fruit. A voice message rings on my phone. An unfamiliar number.

"Dad. It's me."

There is so much crackling static and distortion in the background. I press the phone closer to my ear.

In the distance I can see dark clouds rolling in fast atop the high range in front of the complex. The highest mountain is called Mt. Moriah.

"I'm experiencing the most intense lightning storm I've ever seen. I've never seen anything like this. It's beautiful."

Then a thunderous crash and silence. I quickly call back the number, but no answer. I keep calling.

"Eli," Mike says, clearly in a state of panic. "The transformer was hit. There's a fire near the maintenance garage."

The storm is moving towards us, blackening the sky. Bolts of lightning flash across the barren landscape. I can see a small brush fire where the coyote has been eating.

"Bring your tools and the extinguisher. Quick."

I run to the shed as my cell phone rings again.

"Hello, Zach is that you?"

There is a loud boom and then his voice.

"Dad, is that you…I am in the desert, Dad. The sunsets here are so beautiful. Love you Dad."

Then a loud bang and the call drops. Before I can process what has happened, another call comes in. It is Mike.

"Our Welcome to Moriah Heights sign is on fire. I called the fire department but they told me it'll be a while. I'm heading over there now. Come quick."

When I arrive the fire has consumed the giant wood sign.

"It took me months to make that baby. Carved it all by hand."

The lights in the complex are flickering on and off.

"I worked so hard on that. *Man*"

As I walk towards the smoldering flames with my extinguisher he grabs my arm.

"Let it go."

"We can still salvage some parts of it."

I notice his eyes well up as he looks up at the dark clouds.

"The rain is coming."

He stares at the burning hunk of wood as it crackles then falls to the ground.

"You OK?" he asks.

"I am."

"Good. I'll call the residents. I'll tell them they'll be without power for a while."

The rain smells sweet as it moves closer and blankets the dry landscape.

"Tomorrow there'll be flowers," Mike says, staring at the flames.

"I'll go and check the transformer."

He grabs my arm again.

"You hear from your son?"

I turn to look at his face.

"Yes, I think I did."

"I knew you would."

A lump enters my throat as the rain falls in a more steady rhythm.

"You hear from your wife?" I say.

He turns away from the fire and looks directly at me.

"I did, Eli. I often do. Listen, there will be a flash flood in the morning. The dry river bed will overflow. The parents that are grieving over their son will relive the horrible tragedy all over again."

The rain is coming down in buckets. It falls over the sign and extinguishes the embers from the smoldering wood.

"He's OK?"

"Yes, I think he is."

"Tomorrow, if the roads aren't washed away, I'll purchase wood for our new sign. While I'm gone you can remove the burnt stones and clear the foundation."

"Sounds good."

"Wait here. I want to give you something."

He walks over to his truck and returns with a leather pouch.

"Take this to the grieving parents."

I open the pouch and inhale the aroma. The fragrance triggers a flood of memories.

"Make them tea and sit with them."

As I turn away and walk back into Moriah Heights, I hear the call and response of a male and female coyote. And I remember the beau geste effect, the way two small voices can intermingle and sound like many, can sound strong.

Little Gem Magnolia

I

In an old cafe on Frenchmen Street in The Faubourg Marigny, a ceiling fan churns, throwing dust into the eyes of an old painting of Madame Rose Nicaud. A man dressed in a black Armani suit with a diamond-tipped cane pulls a chair up to the table where I sit writing. He excuses himself for interrupting and offers me a glass of sparkling water.

"Care for a twist-a-lemon with that?" he says.

On his index finger he wears a voodoo Legba ring indicating he's an intermediary—a guardian at the gate of the spiritual crossroads. I know what it is. A leather pouch hangs from his shoulder. I'd seen him once preside over a ceremony at the Louisiana Voodoo Spiritual Temple. He'd spoken about gris-gris amulets, charms and dolls used by enslaved Africans to cast spells on their wicked owners. Stories had emerged about drownings under mysterious circumstances, strange injuries. As disease and the child mortality rate increased, enslaved persons had found comfort and solidarity in their rituals, in the abilities and consciousness they honed. He'd spoken about the powers of Voodoo Queens and their influence on the city of New Orleans. He'd rambled on in English so onlookers and tourists could understand before switching to Creole. I remember hearing something about a Lil' Queenie rising. It hadn't made much sense at the time, but I'd stayed and listened 'till it was over.

"Ayva's hurtin'" he says, folding his arms and leaning across the table. "It's unclear to her why you don't tell your wife. She says you'd be lying to yourself if you don't."

He opens his pouch. Amulets and little charms spill out over the marble surface, his eyes burning like paprika on roasted almonds. The contents of the bag catch and magnify the light of the dim room.

"It would be unfair after all she's done for you."

Directly behind his head, up against the large window, an overgrown banana tree bends from the weight of its fruit, its leaves yellow from stress. He moves his chair closer. I smell the fragrance of her lemon-magnolia perfume in the fibers of his coat.

"Y'know her visa's running out," he says, as he signals to the waitress for another glass. "She can't wait around here forever."

I turn my head and look back at the painting of ol' Madame Rose, patron saint of this establishment. A former slave who saw opportunity despite all odds stacked against her, grabbed what she wanted and took it. I take a moment to absorb this scene and all that's happened to me over the past year, and wonder to myself if this is about us, and a lifetime collaboration together, or about her visa.

"Her homeland's turning into a dictatorship," he says, tapping second line syncopated rhythms with his shoes. I don't think he's able to sit still, always holding the rhythm alive in his body. "She goes back, she'll get squeezed. There's no need for a woman with her talents in a country like that. Here, she's the most sought-after tattoo artist in the crescent city. Y'know my daughter uses her exclusively. She pays top dollar for her illustrations. My daughter's not the only one. If she goes back, her wild spirit and creative juices will get all rung out. Artists 'r always the first to get crushed when 'da walls cave in."

The waitress sets another glass on the table. He slides the lemon wedge from the rim of the glass and closes his large fist around it.

"You want some of this?" he says, watching the juice drip slowly into his glass.

I shake my head, feeling a growing wave of unease in me I can't shake.

"She makes you happy, right? She inspires your photography, right? Your art and all. Yesterday, I had some business in the French Quarter. Afterwards, I was walking up Decatur St. to get a Po' boy and saw her unmistakable face hanging on the walls of your gallery. You were busy bullshittin' with someone who just made a purchase so you didn't see me. But those black and white portraits of her are so beautiful. I almost cried. The world's at your feet. This is your moment, and all because of Lil' Gem Magnolia."

His eyes seem to dance when he mentions her other name.

"Y'know she was left for dead by this guy who was doin' bad stuff to her. She got a big scar to prove it. You must've touched it, I'm sure?"

He rolls up his jacket sleeve exposing the underside of his wrist.

"Even convinced me to get a little one."

The floorboards creak as he pulls his chair closer.

"Y'see we learned from each other—this world ain't so bad if you just make some time."

He looks up at the old photo, removes the Legba ring from his finger and lays it on the table.

"She's comin' to us for dinner tonight. What'll I tell her?"

II

It was midnight,
the first time

an inbound streetcar near Canal Street
turned
before heading uptown

at Common Street
she hopped on,
white blouse covered in red ink stains

and her eyes
flashing
like carnival beads.

We ride along St. Charles under a canopy of live oak,
past Louisiana, Napoleon and Jefferson.

To the bend at the levee.

Her arm brushed my shoulder,
as she rose to pull the cord for her desired stop.

The buzzer still rang through my ears at South Carrollton

near the river,
dark and still.

III

I rise
early

a warm breeze
curls 'round a magnolia tree

lemon fragrance floats
through open windows

painted on her olive skin
a bayou sunrise

tendrils of Spanish moss
cling to a bald cypress tree

and like a blind man gifted sight
I see her journey
from the inside out

bougainvillea creeps
through wrought iron

azaleas explode
with the promise of spring

'look at the river,' she says, lips barely parting

in the present tense
a new story
rising

high tide near the levee

little gem magnolia
offering rare
midnight bloom

IV

A creeping fog curls out of the river
sliding through alleyways,
settling under street lamps.

A river barge turns,
a massive wake swells
water up near Decatur Street.

I walk over worn cobblestones
gilded silver by moonlight
rubbed smooth by my desperate search for Ayva.

Her favorite band is playing at Tipitina's,
I hop the streetcar uptown
There's a good chance she'll be there

Tonight I'll tell her—I'm ready to settle,
to leave my other world behind.

I recognize the bartender and yell to him over the music,

"Hey, where y'at—you see Ayva?"

"She was here earlier. Had a lot to drink. She started dancin' with this stiff looking guy in a black suit. Had this man bag hangin' off his shoulder. She said she got some gig on a river boat, or a barge, celebrating her last night on land. Honestly, her story didn't make much sense, but man, you should've seen her dance. Cleared the floor for a while. She wanted another drink, but I gave her water, instead. Looked like she was wilting from da' heat. Dehydrated and totally wasted. Why you lookin' for her?"

Like white petals against bright green foliage
it's there, if you look.

In winter the bud rots, leaving only memory of nocturnal fragrance
chasing the idea of what was.

Dust settles thick on my camera's lens.

A year will go by
and another,

'Always looking for her,' I tell him. 'Wouldn't you be?'

I walk along Tchoupitoulas Street
to the bend at the river.

I listen to the rhythmic pulse of waves against levee walls
and feel a magnetic pull.

Mystery surrounds me,
like creeping silt in the basin.

The smell of jasmine is sweet.

In the distance a massive ship labors to turn,
unable to navigate through sediment.

And I see Ayva stumbling toward me,
her eyes peer through the dense fog.

In one hand she holds a white dress,
stained with red ink

in the other,
a bucket and shovel.

Portrait of Unknown Woman: Coney Island

I.

While riding the F Train bound for Coney Island, I notice a woman facing me. Although her features are familiar, I can't place where I know her from, or if I know her at all. She moves her head up and down in a metronome rhythm as I slip on my glasses for clarity. I notice her eyes move without seeming to see anything, as if she is mulling something over, or going over some past sequence of events in her mind, but remaining unable to make a connection. When she looks at me, I quickly turn away.

II.

During winter, Coney Island's desolate beach and boardwalk offer great opportunities for photographs. The darkness takes on new depth in ways I can't explain with words, but which are clear to me through my camera's lens. I checked the weather before leaving, then confirmed with my subject to meet me at our designated spot near the boardwalk.

My idea for this shoot is to set my subject halfway between the breaking waves and my tripod. Using the ethereal gloaming of the winter sky as backdrop, my subject, dressed in a dark sweater dress, will contrast as the delicate rays of the winter sun pass through thin clouds. The cold wind whipping on her face turns her light skin red. If all goes well the subject will appear frozen-like with only the fire glow from her charcoal eyes illuminating the photo and echoing the dark water crashing in just behind her. Miranda, my subject for this shoot, was recommended by a colleague at the university. She was a model for her studio art classes. During our meeting the week before at the Cobble Hill Cafe, I showed her my portfolio, and we discussed the shoot. We exchanged ideas about makeup and hair and she suggested certain outfits which might suit what I was after. Jokingly she suggested a series of nude winter shots at the frozen beach. I told her it was the clothes covering the nude I've always found most interesting. On the side of her face above her eye was a pretty deep scar. I could see it underneath a layer of makeup which only made it more visible to my eye. When she caught my eyes scanning her face she quickly sat up, turned to the side and leaned so her hand rested over the blemish. These small details make no difference to me as an artist. My interest lies in illusions, and in perceptions, not some facile idea of perfection. I place my subjects in the middle of what appear to be storms, or representations of turbulence. I direct them to try to appear calm and relaxed as they look at my camera and imagine the viewer looking back at them, wondering what is happening beyond the frame that enables their calm in the apparent storm. What dangers have they known which have taken away their fear? My desire is to capture the subject at that moment of transition. The fine line between an oncoming disaster and the place of better understanding. The surrender. As long as I can control the variables, the imperfections of the subject add to the success of a composition, especially in this case: evidence of harm Miranda had endured which she'd survived. She didn't need to try to hide it from me. But I didn't tell her this.

III.

When the subway door opens, two people shoot up and quickly exit, leaving me alone with the woman across from me. I think about asking her if I look familiar. My curiosity is getting the best of me, to the extent that I decide to speak to her. I gather my things and sling the weighted backpack over my shoulder. I step casually over to the stanchion, halfway between where I sit and where she is sitting. She wears a heavy knitted scarf, and a black sweater dress with black tights and suede boots. Like a makeshift headband, her gold-rimmed sunglasses push her hair away from her face. I notice the socket around her right eye is bruised. On her lap she balances three overstuffed plastic bags tied tight. Each one has only a tiny piece of plastic sticking out from the knot she uses as a handle. Between her and the subway door is an empty baby stroller. I feel like I am trying to recall the end of a bizarre dream. I clutch the pole tightly and watch her movements for clues. She tilts her head to one side as she looks up and sees me staring at her. With a slow, deliberate movement, she lowers her sunglasses over her eyes and leans over to grab the stroller. One of the bags falls to the floor. I step forward and reach down for it where it sits at her feet and offer it to her. She reaches out her hand and takes it.

IV.

The meeting with my student from my Photography Composition Class left me uneasy. I sent her an email warning her that the university had certain expectations. Missing 12 of 16 classes would require me to fail her.

In my email I explained that she'd have to pull an A+ on the final exam for me to even consider giving her a D- for a final grade. At best, that would allow her not to have to pay to do the class again. I checked the University's Health Department website to see if mental illness challenges exempted her from attending classes in person. She replied to my email and requested a meeting to explain her situation. Because of the expense, she couldn't live in the dorms. She and her boyfriend lived near the subway but it would take her two hours to drop their kid off at her friend's house near Coney Island, then take two trains from there to arrive at school. If planned in advance it was possible, but her partner always had their car and never communicated with her as to when he would be home. He worked for the Metropolitan Transit Authority. He would get texts at all hours about downed power lines and switch problems and never knew when he'd be home. With increased storms, the texts became more frequent. I thought of Miranda with her dark eyes against the waves crashing in behind her. When the boyfriend finally arrived back at their apartment, he wanted to go to sleep. He said he was not available to look after their two-year-old son. Last Thursday, the morning of the review for the class's final project, he pulled up after a late-night emergency and forgot his cell phone at the repair site. She was fuming and insisted on taking the car. All he needed to do was call and she'd arrange to have her best friend, Anna, look after their son. Anna was a fashion model from the Czech Republic so only worked a few days a week. She loved looking after their son, and sometimes he would call her *maminka*, mommy in Czech. She thought that was so cute. Her boyfriend said that university is for liberals, and they no longer run the country. He wanted her to quit playing games with useless learning and get a job to help with rent. He said she was failing most of her classes anyway, so if she pulled out now, they could recoup some of the tuition. Rent was already a week late. It would help. He had his own bank account and she never understood with all this late-night overtime why rent was a week late. They argued and she insisted he stay awake and look after their son. She'd take the car and on the way home would pick up his cell phone. While calling his number to find out if the crew had found the phone, he yelled at her to put it down. He insisted that she not take the car and said he was going to sleep. Feeling empowered by the realization that the end was near, she called. She resisted when he swiped at the phone to grab it out of her hands. After a struggle she pulled the phone away from his grip. It slammed into her face causing a gash above her eye. She called. A woman answered in a whispering tone. She was home and he could come by anytime. The voice had an accent. It sounded like Anna.

V.

The cell phone vibrates in my pocket. I wrap my arm around the subway pole to steady my balance, slip it out and tap the screen. It is a text from Miranda. Her train is being held up because of switch problems. They made an announcement that emergency crews are working on it but it could take some time. She apologizes and will text me once it starts moving. She is sitting in a tunnel in the dark, she says.

VI.

My student leaned across the desk, pushed her sunglasses through her hair and adjusted them atop her head. A small band-aid stretched across a gash closing the two parts of skin. Her one eye was blackened and badly bruised. When she caught my eyes scanning her face, she quickly straightened her back, then asked me for one more chance. If I awarded her that and let her present the final project, she promised it would be like no other I've ever seen.

VII.

After taking the bag from my hand, the woman with the stroller doesn't really acknowledge my gesture, just tucks it between her belly and the other two bags. It is at that moment I remember an article I've read a few weeks before. It is about the butcher-on-the-bus phenomenon. It involves a distinction on episodic memory between familiarity and an unsubstantiated impression that an event was experienced previously. Sometimes we can recollect some information on the episode in both the space and time in which it was acquired. The butcher-on-the-bus phenomenon occurs when one believes that a person is familiar upon seeing their face in an atypical context, like the common butcher we see all the time in his store but when we see him on a bus, out of context, we fail to recall any information about that person whatsoever. I often experience this when I see my students outside the classroom. I know that they sit in the third row from the left, usually wear baggy pants and always blurt out the answer. But if I see them dressed more formally in their work clothes, out of the classroom context, I absolutely cannot place them.

VIII.

As promised, the photo series she presented in class for the final exam was nothing short of a work of profound art. The other students who attended my classes on a regular basis presented work that was expected. Compositions which exploited the latest technology, but did nothing to elevate the art of photography, or deepen an understanding of the human condition. I'd have to give them good marks as they did what I asked for, but nothing about any of it was surprising or fresh. However, my failing student's work could end up in a Chelsea gallery. She recreated scenes from her 'messed up life,' which became the name of the series. Each of the 12 compositions told the story of why she was unable to make it to my classes. Some of the photos were violent, some were quirky, but collectively she created a window into the dark world she lived in. The first photo in the series introduced three subjects sitting around a table playing cards. They would be interspersed throughout the rest of the series. The first photo was titled *the cards I've been dealt*. I sensed that she showed me in her compositions what she couldn't tell me at our meeting. It's as if she laid out her cards on the table, and now it would be up to me to decide. On my way from the class to my office I thought about my work at the university. Was my responsibility to the department head? She mentioned it would be a bad precedent to pass a student who barely showed up. She said it wouldn't be fair to the other students who participated in all my classes. I understood this, of course. But what if she was the next Nan Goldin or Diana Markosian? Did I have a responsibility to her as an artist superseding my role as her professor? I could imagine attending her opening at a gallery.

As I walk over to her, she turns to her friends and says to them that he was my professor, and... It was up to me to decide what the next line was. I looked back at the email about the policy towards attendance and grades. It was vague enough. I slipped on my reading glasses and leaned in close to the first photo of the three women playing cards. They struck me as sisters. Each one had a cut above a bruised eye. An email suddenly appeared in bold letters reminding us we had three days to get our grades in. I looked back at the photo to find some flaw to justify something less than an A+. There was none.

IX.

The train slows as it lazily pulls into the last stop. She gathers her three bags and puts her hand on the stroller. I think about helping her by moving the stroller closer to her seat, but my body stays affixed to the pole. It is at that moment a bright flash of sunlight pours in through the dirty train window and illuminates her face. A moment of episodic recognition moves through my temporal lobe. I close my eyes for a moment to let the process of recollection set in. I need to stay focused and let it fully develop before it flies out to the ether and beyond my grasp. A vision passes through me as I remember seeing her on a stage. The warm colored spotlight bathed her face in a soft ethereal glow. Her hair was pulled back off her face. She balanced a fiddle between her chin and shoulder as she looked out at the audience. Her charcoal eyes settled on me watching her as she played. A swirl of music poured from her strings as powerful as crashing surf.

X.

Before submitting my final grades, I laid out her 12 photos across my conference table. I texted a colleague I trusted to come in and let me know what she thought. She lifted the last photo to get a closer look, then turned back to look at me as I waited for her response. She loved how the student put her own life on view. The honesty of what she revealed was painful. She wondered where one goes from here? How is it possible for anyone to leave this mess and focus on their studies? She lifted up one of the photos. It showed a mother holding a child while standing knee deep in garbage. One foot was shackled by a chain that was attached to a pipe under the kitchen sink. I explained to her that it was problematic because the student barely came to any classes. She leaned in closer to the last photo in the series and said it supports the idea that great artists don't need teachers. It's a waste of their time. They just need a school on their artist bio and more opportunities to exhibit. The wall clock indicated a few minutes before noon. I gathered the photos and slipped them into my overstuffed backpack between my camera and tripod.

XI.

We pull into the high modern shed of the renovated train station alongside a replica facade from the old Coney Island station. Like the laying on of

God's giant hands over me, the grand terminal opens as a greeting structure for the curious going into a modern illusion of America's Playground. Balancing the weight of the three bags, she rises from the bench and grabs onto the flimsy stroller. She turns her head towards me as a pulse-like signal runs through my visual cortex. I drop quickly to my knees and withdraw the 12 photos. I flip through them to the last one and hold it in front of me. The last photo in the series shows a woman exiting through a door and pushing a stroller with one hand. In front of her stretches a long desolate boardwalk. The subject is directed to jump straight up in the air but not to let go of the stroller handle. Her hair is tied in a bun so it does not fly up. This gives the illusion everything is normal except she is elevated 12 inches from the boardwalk's wood planks. As she jumps she turns her head slightly toward the camera. We see only half of her face. The sky is overcast but a single ray of sunlight illuminates the woman's one eye. The one parameter for their final project was all photos had to be shot using natural light. What she achieved with limited sunlight took patience and a commitment to small details which made a transcendent composition. I watch as the woman with the stroller crosses the street. Suddenly, as if out of nowhere, golf-ball-like chunks of hail beat down on the street. She doesn't change her gait to hurry and get to shelter but keeps walking with her bundles and stroller. The battering sound on the roof of the grand terminal grows more intense. Like in a metronome rhythm she climbs the ramp to the empty boardwalk. With the food stalls and cotton candy stands shuttered and closed for winter, the balls of ice falling from the ominous sky look like a scene from the apocalypse. As I walk out from the protection of the Stillwell Avenue overpass, I withdraw my cell phone from my back pocket. The hail pounds my head as the 12 photos flash like Tarot cards through my visual cortex. I watch the familiar woman turn left onto the desolate boardwalk and finally out of my vision. I send the last final grade to my department head. As I look up at the wall mural of Grandma's Prediction Fortune Teller, I receive a text from Miranda that the woman who was planning to take her place for the shoot is cancelling at the last minute. She doesn't want to be out in this weather and has to get to her band's rehearsal on time and it all is just too much. She is still stuck on the F train but called another friend who lives in Coney Island. She is coming back from university and is probably already there. She is not a model but a student of photography and very comfortable in front of the camera. She needs the money so will do it in this weather. Miranda tells her to meet me on the boardwalk next to the cyclone. She is picking up her son at the father's girlfriend's apartment at 4pm, Miranda writes, so she might be with a stroller. If I keep my eye out, I should be able to see her.

Netflix Thriller

We watched the documentary called *Free Solo* about the guy who climbed El Capitan with no ropes always one finger grip away from death glued to our computer screen for two hours without moving as the next American hero begins his ascent and remember the climber's girlfriend with wide eyes and wispy hair trembling with fear knowing at any moment it might be his last and wondered how it would look as the camera team shouted oh god while his helpless body fell to the beautiful valley floor but that didn't happen so we watched the Netflix thriller that is all the rage and in real time the hottest thing since *Free Solo* where a marine soldier somewhere in the Middle East has a camera attached to his helmet so the viewers can follow him with his unit on a search and destroy mission as they penetrate deep into villages looking for this enemy sniper who put a piece of shrapnel into their platoon leader's cheek and how we watched as he went down holding his eye and the soldier who had the camera on his helmet said oh god but we didn't think a marine should shriek like that while our tongues burned from eating our favorite chili glazed popcorn that we break out when binge watching and hope today will be the day they find the sniper and sit frozen in suspense with curved spines at the edge of our couch staring wide eyed into the computer screen waiting as our hero appears to make a wrong turn down a deserted street and feel we are right there with him when he enters an abandoned villa our hearts racing as we are sure that he has walked into the crosshairs of a sniper and wonder if our latest American hero might go down today and how cool it is when a spiraling piece of lead enters through kevlar like in slow motion and the body slowly jerks back from the force of the bullet and our hero goes down his body bouncing off the intricate patterns of the tile floor like rubber balls but then we are reminded that this is a reality show and slow motion is off bounds so we scoop our hands into the hot chili popcorn bag feel the burn like pepper spray in our digestive tracts then hear the sound of a bullet whistling and a thud like a car hitting a wall his helmet bouncing over broken tiles spreading blotches of dark red blood as it rolls then silence and we say oh god then lick our fingers as a blurred nothingness is frozen on our screen and tear open another bag just in time to catch episode one of the new comedy series about a group of ivy league students who succumb to the academic stress and devise creative ways to end their lives.

Big Game

A lion wanders through tall grass and spots a female kudu drinking at the edge of a swollen river. Sensing a presence, the cow lifts her head and noses the air. Her fine white stripes are illuminated by the setting sun. The lion sinks to the ground on his haunches patiently waiting for the right moment to strike. When the gorged cow lumbers past the lion he lunges like a bullet in the open air swiping at her backside. The injured cow narrowly escapes and scampers back to the herd. She is wounded. Knowing her fate is all but sealed, the family separates, leaving the compromised animal vulnerable and exposed. Locked in its predatory game the hungry lion chases its prey and again reaches his massive paws for her back legs. She falls to the ground. The helpless kudu turns her head to watch the lion tear through her hide. Steam from their two mouths mixes with the cool evening air. Climbing atop her convulsing body the lion locks his massive jaw into her neck. The kudu exhales her final breath as the African sun sets beyond the horizon.

I'm sitting at a bar gazing at another Cape Town sunset. Now that my novel is finally done, I'll tell Erica that our relationship is over. This book was more difficult than the others. They just don't get easier from one to the next. There are always new issues to grapple with. This one, I had to burn through eight iterations of the first chapter while building out the main character. He was a complex dude. A handsome man child with a huge ego. He plowed through social situations preying on the vulnerable to get what he wanted. I came pretty close to setting him up to be trapped at the end, but like I try to do with all of my work, my signature is to play on the reader's impressions with a subtle twist. Never what they expect, and then I let them make the final assessment. My hope is they'll think, 'holy shit, that's not what I expected.' Was he a hero or something else? Erica was torn over my choice for the last line of the book, "Hey, we all have to eat." After what the main character did, she thought it vile. That she was torn indicated to me I'd done what I'd hoped.

As a confidant and reader of my drafts, this farewell will be more challenging than others. I'll have a few drinks before I do the deed, to numb the pain, my pain.

"Be careful," her ex-husband had said, when we bumped into him and his friends at a Wine Estate near Stellenbosch.

I remember his breath smelled rancid as he leaned in close to warn me. His eyes rolled back and seemed to remain that way for longer than was usual. He was tall and well-built with a shock of blonde hair. Looked like a surfer even though I knew from Erica he was nothing of the sort. His friends joked with him as they scurried away.

"You should have taken him down," I heard one of them say. "She was the best thing in your life."

His warning struck me. I reminded myself he hadn't been talking directly to me, it only felt like it. She had a petite frame and looked much younger than her 36 years. She was a gentle being and in no way was she capable of causing harm. She didn't deserve the hurt I knew she had coming, the hurt I'd cause. I was no newbie to the wildlife of being a single man on the prowl. It'd been a pattern for me for as long as I can remember, though now, closing in on fifty, I was wearying of this cycle I kept traveling. That night I laid awake in bed. I recalled the way his drunken eyes rolled back as his foul breath made me turn away. I wondered what could have made him say that. I wondered about the rest of the history there I didn't know, and never would.

My penchant for traveling to different places and using the land for setting has been a good formula for my books so far. When the opportunity presented itself to leave New York City for a year, I leaped at it. The university where I taught would hold my adjunct position until I returned. Other than that, I was not tethered to anything except my drinking buddies. They'd also hold my position at the bar until I returned. I chose South Africa. I had a few friends living in Cape Town, and I'd never been, which was all the reason I needed. I'd always been in awe of Table Mountain, the wildlife, and the proximity to two great oceans. Also a plus: the U.S. dollar goes quite a long way over there. I could live like a king for the year. This is what I'd been thinking.

I met Erica at a local watering hole my first night in Cape Town. She was at the bar with a big group of her friends. They were celebrating her divorce. I'm still torn about holding a celebration over such a thing, but I guess if one doesn't have kids who the fuck cares. I remember thinking they were a good-looking bunch of women. Mostly blue-eyed, blonde, and

Afrikaans. One turned and asked me if I was from around here. I answered emphasizing my New York City accent and they all turned toward me. There was a moment of quiet as they assessed my foreignness.

"You attached?" one of them said, laughing, though I understood the question was serious.

"Actually I'm not."

"I'll give you a million rand if you marry me. But you'll have to take me away from this continent. I can deal with New York."

Their Afrikaans accents and slurred speech made it tough for me to follow what they were saying.

"Don't listen to them," Erica said. "They wouldn't last a month out of these parts."

After her third glass of wine Erica asked me to drive her home. Her apartment was located on the side of a mountain facing the Atlantic. She lit a joint and handed it to me as we stepped onto her balcony. I remember the moon was full and bright that night. She hoisted herself onto the railing overlooking the vast ocean. I leaned into her warm body and kissed her. She wrapped her hand around the back of my neck and pulled me close.

"I'm unprotected," she said.

The weed, wine and pull of the moon hit me all at once as Erica guided me to her sweet spots. She whispered something to me in Afrikaans but I was so gone at that point I could care less what it meant. In a timed rhythm I felt tiny puffs of hot breath on my cheek. I took her hand to go inside to her bed.

"It's Africa," she said, yanking me back to the balcony. "No one gives a shit."

The silhouette of Table Mountain rose up behind her like a great lurking shadow. Rays from the big moon shimmered off the ocean and illuminated her naked body. I felt her hands push down gently on my head as she guided me to my knees.

"What's that sound?" I said, as the jet lag rolled through me like a gathering storm.

"Some animal. Don't worry."

And that was the last thing I remember from that night.

Hungry to finish in a year, I plowed through an outline, then worked through ideas of the best writing style to create tension. Originally, I toyed with the idea of a third-person narrator, but after I met Erica I was able to tell the story from a close first-person.

"I like where you're going with this," she said after reading the outline. "You can use my name in the story if you want."

I took her advice and changed the original name. Each time I typed Erica it felt like digesting a warm cognac after a good meal. A slight burn as it churned its way through my stomach. How had she understood how helpful this would be to me? The narrator would act as tour guide showing the reader the wild country. It was important that the reader was so close to the action they could feel the breath of the characters whether they be talking, drinking or in the throes of passion. After ten months of long days, I was ready to drop the first draft of my manuscript in the waiting hands of my confidant and main character, Erica.

"The let's-remain-friends thing is a bit cliché," said Erica, her sweet breath encircling my imagination.

"Read on. The tone changes."

So when I end it with her I'll be direct. Something like, 'it's been great, we shared so much together but my publishers are calling me back to New York.'

"I can come with you," she might say.

I've learned what works best for me is to navigate the pressures of publishing deadlines alone in my box-like New York City apartment. Like a hunter watching the shell sail towards its target, I don't want anything to get in the way of the final process. The pressure works for me.

"You want another drink?" the bartender said.

Before I could answer I felt my cell phone vibrate in my pocket.

"Hello, Michael?"

"Yes."

"This is Liz."

It took me a few seconds to connect with the name.

"This is your editor's assistant."

"Oh yes, Liz, hi."

I slid off the barstool and landed both feet firmly on the floor.

"I saw the 212 area code and figured it was Diane calling."

I walked over to the large window facing east.

"I understand. I am using our work phone."

The sky was deep red as the last ray of sunlight disappeared behind Table Mountain.

I would miss the mountains here. I knew this already.

"I'm looking forward to Zooming tomorrow."

"Yes. I'm calling to confirm but also to say that Diane will not be there."

Her voice was dead monotone as if there was some strange disconnect.

"What d'you mean?"

"She's having, uhm, personal issues she has to deal with."

Her voice cracked for the first time.

"Oh no. I'm sorry to hear this. What's going on?"

"She's going through a rough patch with her husband at the moment."

I stepped outside into the courtyard. The area was dimly lit with party lights that wrapped around thick yellow wood tables. Each tabletop had one of the big five South African animals burned into it. I lingered at the lion.

"I'm done with the first draft," I said, crouching onto the wood bench. "Who is going to read it?"

"We're working on it. Rest assured, it will be read."

I pressed my index finger into the carved valley of the lion's mane.

"Can she get it together to Zoom at least?"

"She's not really OK for tomorrow."

I looked up to the dark sky and the silhouette of the looming mountains in the distance.

"I'm not sure I get what's happening."

"She went to surprise her husband on a business trip and that's when it started."

"What started?" I said.

"I should say, ended."

"I'm not following any of this."

"She caught her husband with someone else."

I opened my hand and placed it on the lion's face.

"They've been together awhile?"

"Six years. I don't know about a Zoom call. She's pretty fragile at the moment."

I took the phone away from my ear and took in a breath of the cool air.

"Vulnerable, you mean?"

"Yes, she is. She has taken a leave of absence. Her world's been turned upside down."

"Hunted."

"Did you say something?"

"No," I said. "Just absorbing all of it."

"Sorry I thought you said something."

"Hey, can you give me her number?"

"I can ask her if she's OK with that, but it's not our policy to give out personal numbers of our associates. But honestly, every time I speak with her she breaks down. Just cries and cries. I'm at a loss."

"I get the situation, but business is business. The publishing house needs to move this forward and I work with her. Get me her number, OK?"

"I'll ask."

I heard chatter in the background and then silence.

"You still there?" I said.

"Sorry, Michael. Can you just hold on a minute?"

I sipped the last drop of warm beer and heard the sound of an animal in the distance. Another thing I'd miss about South Africa: the wildlife in shared spaces, the sense of the human and animal realms right next to one another, often overlapping. I thought again of Erica. I'd gotten used to making love with her outdoors. When I hear sounds of wild animals or even a breeze from the ocean blowing over me, I get aroused. I imagine she is setting the table and wondering where I am. It's a shame her fate is sealed, but…

"Michael?"

"Still here."

"Ok, here's what we can offer," she said.

"You spoke to her?"

"I did not."

"You said, *we*?"

I heard faint mumbling in the background.

"Right. We feel it is best if you work with me. We don't know if she is coming back."

I stood up and walked to the edge of the courtyard. I could hear the crashing waves in the distance.

"I'll take over from Diane. I feel terrible for her but she is really vulnerable at the moment. I don't think she can be trusted to make good decisions."

"Her instincts are the best."

"I understand, but my record shows I am as capable as Diane."

I looked up at the starry Cape Town sky and thought about the challenges of working with another editor. The intimacy of someone else diving into my body of work, ripping it apart and slowly reassembling it was reserved for Diane. It takes a steady hand and the focus of a sharp shooter to work with me and my ego. She's the only one.

"Sorry, Liz. My allegiance is with Diane. And, frankly, the contract, too. Honestly, I don't think I'll have the same success with you or any other editor. It's not personal. I have no doubt you're capable."

The muffled voice in the background became louder.

"Who are you talking to?"

"The president of the company. I'm relaying your demands."

Demands. I liked that. After 4 books, one a best seller, I'd arrived. I had clout, *Gravitas*. I walked back to the table with the carving of the lion and looked around at the other images of the Big Five. Elephant, Rhino, Cape Buffalo, Leopard, and of course, the Lion. Erica told me that for South Africans they represented the most challenging mammals to hunt because they were known to be dangerous. It was considered a feat by trophy hunters to bring them home and hang their heads over the bookshelves. Now it's all about just seeing them. A checklist of sorts of what to do while in South Africa.

"Michael?"

"Yeah, I'm still here. Got her number?"

"Uhm, well, you signed a contract with Wellspring Publishing."

I pushed the phone closer to my ear to make sure I'd caught the words correctly.

"Can you say that again? I kinda lost you for a moment."

"You have a contract with us, and there's no clause indicating which editor it might be from project to project."

I raised my hand to catch the attention of the server.

"Get me another beer," I said, holding the phone away from my face as I handed the mug to her. "And a shot of whatever goes with it."

"Right away, sir."

I watched her gait as she sprinted off to the bar.

"You mentioned a contract?"

"Yes, I did, Michael. And the contract is with Wellspring Publishers, not with Diane."

The server arrived and placed my drinks on the coasters.

"So you're saying that I have to work with whoever Wellspring gives me."

The shot burned my throat as it flowed through my stomach.

"Yes, Michael. You are under contract to finish the first draft in a year. Unfortunately, due to these unforseen circumstances, Diane won't be able to finish the work she started, but you still have to complete the draft and work with whomever we assign to work with you to bring it to completion. I do understand this might be unsettling, but I want to give you my word that I'm fully able and determined to step in here."

I put the glass of beer to my mouth and didn't stop drinking until it was finished. The cold liquid soothed my burning throat. I found I had nothing left to say.

"I know it's late and you're probably out drinking…"

"I'm out but why do you say drinking?"

"Well, Diane has told me about you."

I raised my glass so the server would notice.

"Another one, sir?"

It took me a moment for my eyes to get into focus and determine it was the same woman as before.

"And a shot."

"Right away, sir."

My cell phone vibrated with a text from Erica.

"I'm waiting for my man," she wrote.

I swiped her message away from the screen.

"Are you still there?"

"Just ordering another drink," I said, accentuating the last word.

"So I know it's late but can you send me the manuscript tomorrow morning, your time?"

I grabbed the shot and downed my beer before the server could lay it on the table.

"I'll consider it," I said, returning the glasses to the tray.

I noticed she was looking into my eyes. I looked back until she retreated, balancing the tray with her one hand.

"I understand."

I was about to hang up and begin the trek to Erica's apartment but my brain, now gorged with alcohol, pushed out some final words.

"Is she still employed with Wellspring?"

There was a pause in her reply and then what seemed like an eternity of silence. I waited patiently for her reply.

"I'm not at liberty to say, Michael."

"She told me she started the company with her husband."

"Yes, that's right."

"So is the owner of the company the one whose dick is out of control?"

"I think we should talk in the morning, your time."

With the alcohol taking over my coherency, I tried one last time to speak in frank words.

"Are you by any chance his new little pussy cat?"

"It's a bit hard to hear you, Michael."

"What I meant to say is if she's still with Wellspring and I have a contract with y'all, then I'll be expecting her call tomorrow at 10 a.m. my time."

"She's getting used to the taste of freedom. Or should I say being alone. She's all about her personal needs at the moment. Now if you'll forgive me, I'm really not able to share more."

"You seem to know a heck of a lot about her personal situation?" I said. "How's that?"

"I am a friend."

"This guy's an asshole, don't you think?"

Another gap of silence seemed to stretch out longer than I expected. It started to feel like I was being stalked by this Liz. She seemed to know too much. I pushed on. Had I been sober, I would have met her silences with those of my own, tried to throw her off balance. But I'd made the decision to drink for a reason. There was an appropriate time for measured calculation and the same for unchecked instinct. I let mine fly.

"Well I signed the contract 'cause the great Diane would be working with me. So as long as she is still with the great Wellspring, I want to, no demand to, work with her. Or, we can have a lawyer figure it all out."

I could feel my chest fill with air.

"What say ye, Liz? Do you still want my manuscript first thing in the morning, my time?"

I rose slowly from the bench and laid out all the cash I had in my pocket. I had plenty. With no response from Liz I took it upon myself to terminate the call.

"I'll bring you the check right away, sir," the server said.

"No need. It's all there for you."

"Should I call for a taxi to take you home?"

The last word reverberated through the African night and lodged somewhere in my present state. I wasn't sure where my home was in that moment.

"I think I'll walk, but thank you."

"I know you are not from around here, sir."

"You're right," I said, turning towards her. "I'm from New York. I'll be fine."

"There's rules in New York," she said. "Please, there are different rules here. You understand."

I pulled my sweater over my head and rearranged my hair.

"Here," I said, pulling out my wallet and handing her an American ten dollar bill.

"You already paid me, sir. Please keep it."

"I insist."

I turned and left, and didn't look back.

I took a shortcut to Erica's apartment through a fairly sketchy part of town. The air felt good as I went through the break-up steps in my head. I anticipated the usual remarks. I'd leave her with the notion that I'd return for a few weeks next year after the book came out. I'd be sure to do a reading tour of the Cape and talk about why I chose this spot to set the book. I cut through a park a few blocks from her apartment and noticed some activity near a small stream running the length of the perimeter. I walked closer and found a family of baboons mulling around something. It was dark and I couldn't identify what it was but looked like something was moving. A homeless family sat near the stream a few meters from the baboons.

"Shu," I heard one of them say.

He threw a stone into the crowd. I heard a knock like knuckles on wood as it landed squarely on the baboon's frontal lobe.

"Get away," he yelled.

I followed the stream out of the park and back out to the street. I looked up at her balcony and remembered our first night together. The screams of the animals and the waves breaking on the shore. I outlined the entire book during that encounter. I'd call the main character Erin. And then the wine and ganja and jet lag hit me, and I passed out.

I'll set my next novel near the coast, work the plot around surfing. I read of a horrible shark attack last week in the Cape Times. I can't get the picture of the victim out of my mind. She was so young. That same week at my local watering hole I met a woman named Erin. She said she knew her. Lived in a cottage next to her in a secluded beach area outside of Cape Town. She knows the area well and offered to take me around and show me the coast and all the wild spots. She asked me if I'm a surfer.

Message (1) Erica 8:11 PM: Where are you? Can you pick up a bottle of wine? I set the table outside. I am removing my clothes. Come quick.

This is how it all started. The first few weeks I couldn't stop texting her. I was hooked. Erin was everything I wanted. Or should I be truthful and use the phrase, everything I needed. So I worked on my novel during the day, met her at night. I checked my phone constantly. I'd text her before my morning run to start the flow of words. I'd be skipping over rocks at the base of Table Mountain imagining her soon-to-be ex-husband reading the text while she was in the shower. I was inspired. After she left him, I started to play a dangerous game. I'd go weeks without answering her texts. It drove her crazy. I'd imagine her roaming the streets at night cursing me. Telling her friends what an asshole I am. I loved it. I sent my draft to the publisher two months ahead of schedule. Hey, we all have to eat.

I let myself into Erica's apartment. She greeted me with a kiss. Her fragrance was sweet and familiar, and it played on my senses. I handed her the revised final chapter to read. My last act before severing ties.

"I can read it tomorrow."

"It would mean a lot if you could read it now. I'll slice the meat in the meantime."

I peeked out from the kitchen to watch her turning the pages. Her eyes were wide as she clamped down. The blood streamed over the cutting board. Small drops fell onto the kitchen floor. She turned to the last page and read it aloud, her voice at a low decibel I'd never heard her use, even at her least inhibited. Her nostrils flared. I walked back into the living room with a piece of meat on a fork.

"Try this."

She rose and tore the papers into pieces and crumpled them onto the floor.

"Get the fuck out."

I pressed against her and squeezed her tight, and I could feel in her body that she accepted the inevitability of this. It was nature's course.

"I love you, Erica. We can remain friends."

She threw her head back and closed her eyes, surrendering.

The nocturnal hunt gives way to the rising sun. Morning light spreads over her naked body, illuminating her deep scars. I tiptoe over to the vanity and write down my thoughts. I carefully fold the paper in half and place the note on the pillow next to Erica's head. A stiff breeze pushes through the open window. I grab my belongings and walk out along the edge of the nearby park. A stream runs through it. A pack of wild dogs run across the plain, on the scent of something. I turn away from the glare of the sun to check my phone for new signs of life. It's morning, my time. It's a new day, a new chase.

The Other Side of the Moon

"I finished editing the photos from our last session," Michael texted.

"How do they look?"

"If we are still on for Saturday we can meet early and have a coffee before the shoot. I'll bring my laptop. You be the judge."

He usually kept his ideas under tight wraps. But with Michelle things were different. She was his first subject in thirty years he'd shared his thoughts and ideas with. He trusted her intuition and looked for clues in her facial expressions when she reacted to his photos. Their connection took him by surprise.

"Tell me why you don't like this one," he said, tapping at his screen.

She sat stone still as if she was trying to remember something. He slid his chair closer.

"Look here. Your shadow is slightly off."

He leaned in closer.

"The shadow should have cut my face on an angle. See how that would be better? There'd be more dichotomy between shadow and light."

He craned his neck and touched the left side of her head. She didn't move.

"Yes. There. It should have come across my face this way."

He followed her finger to the screen as he inhaled the fragrance of her—how had he not noticed this before? She smelled of cedar, of deep woods.

"Yeah, I wasn't so crazy about it, either."

He arched his back and rested his chin in the palm of his hand.

"Hey, I finally got to see Dara's exhibit," he said, turning toward the side of her face and focusing his gaze on her barrette.

She set down her coffee cup and turned her head away from the screen. Like a magnet, her eyes locked into his as she reached up to secure her barrette, as if she'd felt his gaze fixed exactly there.

"What did you think?"

***

Michelle's interest in Michael's photography started the previous year. She had arrived early to a meeting at a print shop her company used and noticed a photography magazine on the table. Michelle was the team leader for a group of graphic designers and had the responsibility of creating fresh ideas for new ad campaigns. Most of the clients were other Jersey Shore companies and music venues. At first, she'd been excited by the possibilities for this work, the potential to be free with her artistic vision. That morning, she'd arranged to meet with the printer to look at options and get a quote. While she waited, she scrolled through a series of texts sent by the owner's son, the vice president. She clashed with him on everything. His taste was hyper-commercial without an ounce of artistic integrity. Michelle bristled as his subordinate and quickly came to understand this position would not involve artistry, but forbearance, frustration.

"You might have an ounce of talent, but I have tons of connections, and guess which of those have the ability to get things done," he'd say.

He was right. The campaigns could never happen without him. He was a hard drinker and cocaine user. He was mercurial, difficult to share space with even for a moment. He had an expensive convertible and lived in one of the glamorous apartments in nearby Red Bank. Everyone down the shore knew him, and knew, too, of his shortcomings of character. Michelle's job was made infinitely more difficult by the need to please him. One day, while working on this new campaign, he raised his voice at her during a meeting with a new client over artistic direction. She remained silent and turned red as she sank into her chair, furious with herself that she'd been so vulnerable as to show her emotion so nakedly. She'd worked for weeks on this new series and was excited about running the meeting. The ideas she presented for the campaign not only touched on themes they were interested in but also showed a creative thread she felt their customers would appreciate.

"I don't think that's what they had in mind, maybe too indirect, I'd say." Danny looked directly at the clients as he spoke and never so much as glanced in Michelle's direction.

"She'll try a few more ideas and see if she can hit on what you're after."

"I think it's there," said Michelle. "Like a *New Yorker* comic, it just takes a moment for that to click. I think we can trust our viewer to get it."

"How long does that take to be captured? They're not looking for art here. They want sales. Will the viewer want to purchase it? You can't forget the point. It's why we're here."

Michelle was infuriated. When she looked down at her cell phone and saw Danny's number, she stuffed it into her pocket. She shifted her attention to a photography magazine laid out on the glass table and tried to breathe. On the cover was a photo of a naked woman on an expansive beach seated in a wooden chair. She wore shiny turquoise high heels. The photographer caught the setting sun just as it shed its light over her face and shoes. The composition was inexplicably eerie, something about the contrast of the soft curves of the naked woman positioned against the stark lines of the wooden chair. In the background thick clouds were brewing, causing the subject to look uneasy as the imminent storm approached. There was an element of fear suffusing the composition.

Suddenly the door opened and a man appeared leaning in on the handle.

"Sorry," he said. "He's still on the phone."

"That's fine. I'm in no rush."

She waited for him to close the door and slid the magazine into her backpack.

***

After work she met with her friends at Wonder Bar.

"Hey Michelle," the bartender said. "You doin' the fliers for the fall shows?"

"I am," she said. "Y'also gonna give me free passes to all of 'em, right?"

"I'll see what I can do."

She grabbed her beer and went to sit with the others at the tiki bar. Like a forged sickle ready to harvest the night, a bright sliver of waxing crescent hung over them.

"Look at this," she said, taking out the magazine from her backpack.

"Wow."

"Fuckin' beautiful, right?"

Michelle flipped to the back page and pointed to the photographer's bio.

"He's from Asbury."

"No way."

"Yes, way, and fuckin' hot."

Her friend grabbed the magazine and squinted her eyes.

"Doesn't say if he's single."

Michelle lifted the magazine away from the grip of her friend between her thumb and forefinger.

"Listen girls, I'm a bit obsessed at the moment."

"He's no youngster."

"Anyone who can put together photos like this needs to be met."

A drip of water fell onto the thin paper.

"I think it's raining," her friend said. "We better go inside. Don't want to get Mr. Hotty all wet."

"That's weird," Michelle said, looking up at the night sky. "My app said clear skies for tonight."

"My app said there is a high chance of getting laid tonight."

Michelle put her arm around her friend as they walked inside.

"Is your app usually accurate?"

"We'll see."

That night after showering, she flopped belly first onto her bed and thumbed through the magazine. His headshot was in black and white. It showed a clean-shaven man with a shock of unruly silver hair. His skin appeared sunburnt and taut. He wore hyper-cool glasses over heavy-lidded eyes. He was a force of nature. She opened the magazine to his photos, set a chair in front of the full-length mirror and removed her clothes.

***

"Dara's show was one of the best conceptual exhibits I'd ever seen," Michael said.

He clicked his mouse to the next photo. Michelle rested her head sideways on the seat of a wooden chair. Her eyes were aligned in a lateral position and opened wide as she gazed outward. She appeared to be relaxed in a natural pose, but her glass-like features and frozen expression could suggest otherwise, belying this apparent ease and creating a tension in the composition.

"I love this," she said, tapping on the screen.

"Me too."

Michelle leaned back in her chair and watched Michael's hand glide across his notepad. His wedding band sparkled as it caught the rays of sunlight beaming through the window. She was excited by their collaboration. Time seemed to stand still as they discussed where she should stand or what emotion she should summon to get the expression just right. The gentle way he directed her was liberating and she reciprocated by offering him numerous poses with slight variations on each. She felt free and respected in her motivations and ensuing gestures.

"That's beautiful," he'd say to her, as he stepped closer.

She dropped her shoulders slightly and released the tension in her face.

"Perfect. Hold, just three more shots."

His decision to share the results with her made a difference. Michelle could tell how her poses would ultimately read on the screen. She was able to understand his vision in a way that gave a directed clarity to each session. As the months went by they began to produce great art. Magazines reached out to Michael offering him full spreads and hefty accompanying checks.

"Don't settle for just the inside," she said, remembering the magazine she found on the print shop table. "These are front-cover worthy."

At thirty-two, a sense of repetition had set in for Michelle. The excitement of her job faded. Lackluster designs with no creative input that enhanced cut-and-paste blurbs were what her man-child boss demanded. Danny would always have the last word and she grew tired of the fight, so day in and day out she just showed up and did as she was told, in it only for the paycheck

"You should tell Danny's boss about his jerk-dom," her friend said.

"That would be his father."

"Then look for another job."

One by one, her friends were also giving up on their once beloved beach community with its quirky bars and nightlife. Unlike Michelle, they were all in serious relationships and looking at marriage as their next big step. Michelle, on the other hand, was balancing on the edge of something she could not quite figure out. Like the gravitational pull of the moon on the waters of the earth, she stood on shifting sands unclear where she'd end up. A storm was gaining strength, and until it settled, she would not know the extent of the damage or what treasures washed up with the tide. The mystery was intriguing and excited her in a way she had not experienced before. She stood still in the uncertainty, eyes wide open to whatever would come next.

She remembered the woman in the photograph who was naked but for the oncoming storm, and her turquoise heels. There was something wonderful about those heels, she thought, something indicating the woman's refusal to live in the realm of the practical, even in the face of uncertainty.

"I'd love to go see the exhibition," she said, sipping her coffee and turning to look directly at Michael.

"What?"

"Dara's exhibit. I'd love to go."

A moment passed as Michelle looked through the cafe window out to the sea. A seabird skimmed the water, then cut it as it snapped its bill on the body of a fish. Michael looked up at the sound of a chair scraping the floor. A slender woman slung her beach bag across her shoulder and pushed down on her wide brimmed fedora. She paused to turn and look out the window. Michael followed her movement as she exited. Michelle turned her attention back to his computer screen and wondered how long their collaboration might last.

"I'd love to see what you see in Dara's art."

Michael turned and caught her staring at him. He pushed down on the arms of the chair and straightened his back.

"Well, I'll be in Chelsea next Tuesday. I have a meeting at noon, but I can meet you afterwards if you'd like?"

The words rolled through the hum of the coffee shop.

"You don't mind seeing it again?"

"It'll be an experience to see it with you."

***

"Sorry I'm late," he said.

"No worries."

"Is that a new jacket?"

Michelle moved her shoulders playfully back and forth as she unzipped her jacket.

"I got here early and did some shopping. You like it?"

"Fits you really well."

She guided her hair behind her ears and moved her head to the side.

"These too," she said, exposing a pair of bright silver earrings.

Like a seabird gliding over open ocean, Michael's eyes darted from her gaze to the heavy, glass door with the name OMAN Gallery written on it and back to her.

"They look great with the jacket."

She looked at her reflection in the glass.

"Thanks. I agree."

Mike stumbled as he stepped back from her magnetic aura. She smiled and pushed open the heavy door. Something was shifting, and she was relishing it, this new sense that a new movement was pushing forward.

"After you," she said, making sure his path was narrow.

"Is this your first time?" a man with an English accent asked from behind the desk.

"It's my first time."

"I've been here before."

He handed each of them a price sheet.

"She's in the gallery so if you need to ask her anything."

Michelle walked to the center of the room.

"Oh my god."

He kept pace alongside her to watch for her reactions.

"Freakin' crazy," she whispered, stepping into the alcoves.

"Yep, she's great," he said, leaning close to her.

He could smell the sharp fragrance of her leather jacket, and that smell of her he recognized now: of pine, the woods at night. Michelle gasped as she looked up at the large photo in front of the makeshift altar.

"It looks like they're crying for help."

In the center of the lobby, a group of people gathered around a woman wearing a bright yellow dress. She pointed to the life-sized photo at the far end of the room.

"This one represents hope. I set her hands this way to give a feeling of someone gathering her disciples and bringing them to a safe harbor."

"Is that her?"

"Must be," Michael said. "Let's go see."

They pressed their way to the edge of the tight circle. Michelle fixed her attention to the woman at the center in the yellow dress. She spoke animatedly, and they all listened.

After the crowd dispersed, the woman walked over to Michael.

"Mikey," she said, opening her arms and smiling.

He leaned into her orbit and they held each other tightly.

"It's been so long. Let me look at you."

She pulled away but didn't let go of his arms, looking him over carefully.

"You don't age."

She glanced over at Michelle.

"Who's this beauty?"

"This is Michelle."

Dara extended her hand.

"It's a pleasure. Your work is amazing."

Dara looked at Michael and motioned with her hand at Michelle.

"She's the subject of a new series I'm working on."

"You have a wonderfully expressive face. I see why he chose you."

Michelle pivoted her feet and turned and squared her body in front of Dara.

"Thank you, but I chose him."

Dara's face was illuminated as she stepped back. Like a solar eclipse, Mike watched as Michelle's dark frame was blocked by the fiery yellow dress. Each was silent as they moved in tandem one a step at a time.

"What do you think of my work?"

"I haven't seen everything yet, but so far I love it."

"I'd love to know your thoughts after you've seen it all."

She pointed to the paper in Michelle's hand.

"My number's on the paper. Reach out to me. I'm curious."

"I absolutely will. It's really nice meeting you."

"Why don't you go on and see the rest of the show," Michael said. "I'll be here. Take your time."

They watched as she disappeared into the next room.

"She's special."

"This is her first time doing this."

Dara rested her hand on his cheek.

"How's Bev?"

"We have our ups and downs."

"You should've married me," she said smiling.

"You want to tell me about your new series?"

"I'm still in the development stage. Nothing concrete yet."

Michelle exited from the alcove, craned her neck and looked up at the high ceilings. She removed her cell phone from her pocket and spoke into it as she walked slowly across the brightly painted floor.

"You'll work with just her," she said, turning towards Michelle. "Or you have others in mind?"

"Just her."

Dara watched Michelle enter the next temple.

"I totally understand. You definitely got something here."

"Yep. I know."

"I'll call you next week. Let's get lunch."

***

They settled into a cafe on 8th Ave. a few blocks from the gallery. The space was modern and airy, with a marble bar.

"Can I get you a coffee or a glass of wine?"

"I normally don't drink wine at this time of day," Michelle said. "But I need to process that experience."

"We'll get two Pinot Noirs," he said to the server.

"She's so cool," said Michelle. "Let's do something like that."

He opened his laptop and opened the file of the last shoot. Michelle sipped her wine and pointed to the screen.

"That belongs in a show," she said.

"There needs to be more."

She leaned back in her chair and looked up toward the string lights draped along the ceiling, so many tiny fixed points of light, like stars in a night sky, reflecting the light of the sun.

"What about this one?"

"I don't know, it doesn't really speak to me."

He jotted down a few notes and moved to the next.

"How 'bout this?"

"I feel her pain."

He pushed back in his chair and crossed his arms.

"Michelle, can I pay you for your work? Art models generally get $200 an hour."

"If you pay me we're not collaborating. Besides, I'm not a model."

He lifted his glass and waited for her to acknowledge.

"Cheers to our creativity."

Her new silver feather earrings danced as she turned to the side and removed her leather jacket, sliding out one arm and shoulder at a time. Once she was free of it, he grasped the collar and placed it across the back of the chair.

"Thanks, partner," she said, raising her glass. "Cheers, to us."

She leaned closer to the laptop and pointed to another photo.

"This is how I felt that day."

He expanded the photo to take up the whole screen.

"I can see that."

She picked up the serrated wooden knife and carefully cut all the charcuterie into perfect halves, for sharing.

"I have an idea."

"Let's hear it."

She rolled a curl of prosciutto onto her fork and slowly placed it into her mouth and chewed.

"What if we shoot based on the eight phases of the moon?"

Michael sipped on his wine and turned his chair to align with hers.

"I prefer shooting in the studio."

"The goal is not to shoot with the moon."

"I'm not really getting it."

"I'm a conduit for the energy of the moon. You shoot me as if I'm the phases of the moon. Each phase has its own distinct frequency"

Michael sipped on his wine and leaned in closer.

"From the time I was a little kid growing up near the shore, I watched the moon from my window or from the beach. You know the moon is essential for birds' migration and navigation patterns. Sometimes their reproduction coincides with the particular phases of the lunar cycle."

"How about you?"

"I'm like the sand hopper. We work very hard to keep ourselves in our ideal waterfront real estate. Without the moon guiding them they'd be dried out on the beach, eaten by sea birds or swept out to sea. They stay buried during the day and can forage efficiently during the night at low tide."

She looked back at the photo on the screen.

"The moon pulls us based on two compasses. One helps with orientation, the other helps with navigation. We have a sun compass in our brain and they have a moon compass in their antennae."

"Amazing. What's your antennae?"

"My feelings. I have intense feelings about things," she said, turning towards him and looking at his bright eyes. "Emotional hyperarousal, they called it."

Michael placed his half of the prosciutto into his mouth.

"I know my body and psyche are affected by the moonlight and its cycle and rotation. I'm like a lunar clock. I want to explore it and really understand it."

"Interesting," he said, nodding as he watched her and waited for her next thought.

"The moon is visible during daylight except when it's in the new or full moon phase because it's too close to the sun to be seen. But the rest of the time the moon should be visible in the morning. My plan is to go to the beach just before dawn."

"What if it's cloudy during the six phases when it's visible during the day?"

"I don't need to see the moon to feel how it impacts me."

She took a last sip of her wine and looked down at her phone.

"My train is at 6."

Michael locked his eyes on her frame as she got up and rotated to the back of the chair to retrieve the jacket he'd placed there just a short time before.

"You know the moon is tidally locked to Earth?"

"I never really thought about it," he said, looking up into her face.

"But because it's not a perfect sphere, as it turns, a smaller portion of the moon moves in toward Earth and a larger portion moves away."

A stream of sunlight broke through the large windows above the bar. She squinted, then moved her head slightly to get out of the rays.

"This uneven distribution in gravity causes a torque, or a rotational force. It makes the moon spring back into place. There's so much of this force affecting every moment of our lives, we just don't always understand the reach of it, or we don't recognize what it is, just a mysterious pull."

He stared at her in silence as she dropped her phone into her bag. Half of her face was now lost in a shadow.

"It's a nice photo with the light on your face."

"You mean the shadow," she said, smiling.

"What's that called?"

"What?"

"That spring-like motion," he said, following her fingers as she zipped her bag.

"Lunar libration," she said, not looking at him.

She shifted the bag over her shoulder and looked down at him where he sat.

"You know we never see the other side of the moon. It's in sync with the earth, so we only see one side."

"I never thought about that. Curious what it looks like."

She expanded her chest to take in a large amount of air as she extended her hand. Michael rose and gently gripped her hand.

"I like your idea."

"Good."

"Which of the 8 phases of the moon will you start at?"

Michelle clutched the elastic band stretched around her ponytail and slowly pulled down.

"New moon," she said, her dark hair spreading in a wide fan across her neck. "Absolutely the new moon."

***

Michelle made a pact with herself that each morning, no matter the weather, she would go through a meditation routine at the beach as the moon traveled on its path. She would use the hour to explore every aspect of herself. From the interior world of her mind to the ebb and flow of the physical world and how it played upon her body. She found her perfect spot among the dunes between the south shore of the Asbury Park beach and the old Victorian town of Ocean Grove. The seabirds were deafening during their early morning feeding hour, creating a wall of urgent sound. Some mornings she would stand on one leg in tree pose. Other mornings, she would mimic the seabirds, balancing her body on one leg with arms outstretched toward the sea. She disciplined herself to hold each standing position on one leg for thirty minutes before switching to the other. She could scream at the roaring waves, speak words aloud or just be silent. Her mood always directed her and she would react, trying not to edit herself too much, just to be present and aware of her primally occurring urges. The one constant was the roaring hum of the crashing ocean against the shore. After her hour-long ritual, she'd walk to the north end of the Asbury boardwalk, grab a coffee and sit beneath the ornate ceiling of the Grand Arcade in the old Convention Hall. She wrote until she finished her coffee. She photographed her pages and saved them in a document. When the month was finished she would share everything with Mike and work with him to plan the shoots.

This morning while meditating on the waxing gibbous, she wrote in her journal, *I thought about the other side of the moon.*

She looked out through the large windows that framed both the boardwalk and the sea. The golden hour of the rising sun ignited half of the interior of the Convention Hall. Decorative lights strung across the ceilings and sides looked like small stars in a great universe. Massive banners with names of bands hung down along the walls. Early morning cyclers, power walkers and curiosity seekers bowed in awe as they entered the great hall, their eyes lifting to the ceiling of the cavernous space. As she removed her phone from her backpack, Dara's business card fell to the ground at her feet. A large seabird landed, pecking at a scrap of food. She thought about how Dara's large scale photos made her uneasy. She scrolled through Dara's

Instagram and commented beneath one of the photos, 'made me uneasy in a wonderful way. Loved the exhibit.'

"You must be a messenger," she said as the bird tore into an abandoned bagel half.

She shifted her attention up to the wall banners, imagining Michael's photographs of her hanging there for the public to absorb.

It moves around Earth at the same rotation so we only see one side, she wrote in her journal. *The other side is mysterious and dark, full of pockmarked craters and valleys slicing through its surface.*

The seabird, finished with its bagel, spread its wings and took off in flight. It glided through the bright hall to the opening at the darker side and out toward the roaring sea.

"But we never see it."

She flipped to the back page of the journal and sketched a self portrait. She drew herself standing on the beach. She looked out at Michael who stood in the water. The moon over Michael's head was a waxing crescent. A sharp stream of light crossed over Michelle's face. At the dark end of the beach standing atop the boardwalk, Dara looked out at them.

"Like me," she said. "We never see it."

A well-built, shirtless man glanced at her lips as he jogged past the table.

"Never."

He slowed his pace as she formed the word.

"Did you ask me something," he said, removing his earbuds.

She interlocked her fingers above her head and stood on her tiptoes.

"No."

Her eyes were drawn to a fresh tattoo laid across the right side of his hairless chest. A singular white light passed through a dark triangle prism and dispersed into a spectrum of colors. Her thoughts drifted to a song whose melody she could not remember. He squared his body in her direction and pointed at his chest.

"No, just talking to myself," she said, moving her lips intentionally, as if his earbuds were still lodged in his canal, then waved him on.

She lifted her cell phone to see a text from Michael.

"How did it go this morning? Any revelations?"

A few things were evident to her, but she wasn't sure she was ready to share them. When the moon was in the waxing crescent her sexual energy increased. During the first quarter, the urge to make physical changes to herself intensified. But this morning was by far the most distinct. The phase of the waxing gibbous channeled her energy to assess relationships and detach from situations she deemed unhealthy. It felt reasoned, intentional.

"I'm halfway done!"

"Haha. Today's the waxing gibbous, right?"

"Yep."

Michelle gathered her things and walked outside. A diver clutching a harpoon, adjusted his mask and walked into the sea. A seabird balanced on the wind at the water's edge looking for crabs.

"Are you free now?"

Michelle hesitated before tapping send.

She watched the three dots undulating through the cloudy, white screen, each one fading then returning like the tide.

"I could be, why?"

She looked out at the wide expanse of water, the limitless horizon of possibility it seemed to represent.

"I'm here," she wrote as another seabird skimmed the water.

"I'm already boarding the train. How about Thursday?"

"Sure."

***

At the end of a sandy street a sun-bleached awning drooped over a pair of lovers. The moon was pale and waning. An intermittent breeze pushed thick, ocean air through large windows at the front of the cafe. Michelle planted her elbows firmly on the bar, wrapping her hands around a candle jar. Michael removed his cell phone from his pocket and placed it next to the jar.

"You just got off the train?"

"I had a drink with the owner of OMAN Gallery before I left the city," he said, reaching for his cell phone.

"I need to get this call," he said and walked to the center of the room.

Michelle glanced to the open windows to see if the moon was still in sight. She heard Michael say he was in a meeting with the owner of the OMAN Gallery at the moment and would be home soon afterwards.

"Something wrong?" she said, the glow from the flickering flame splashed over her face. He turned away from her eyes, lifted his glass to his lips and sipped his red burgundy.

"No. All good."

"It's good to see you," she said.

"You too. What did you want to meet about?"

She unbuttoned her cardigan sweater and placed it on the back of the bar seat. She turned her back toward him and lowered her short strap.

"Very cool," he said.

He took another sip of wine then rested his finger next to the tattoo. Instead of pulling away, she raised her left hand and met his hand on the top of her shoulder.

"I designed it myself."

The tattoo showed each phase of the moon resting between the offshoots of a leafless, winter branch. The branch curved around her shoulder blade with the full moon in the center. The three inch, single color composition was the only illustration on her body.

"It's beautifully eerie," Michael said.

"That was my intention."

"You gonna do more?"

She turned, squared her body in front of his frame and reached for her drink.

"Do you have a dollar?"

"I do."

"I want to take a photo in the photo booth of my back with my tattoo."

Michael stood up on his toes to let the electric surge pushing through his body run its course.

"Come with me," she said, holding out her hand to him.

She entered the booth and removed her shirt.

"No peeking."

She looked out below the curtain where Michael was standing.

"Unless you want to come in and help me get positioned?"

There was a long moment of silence.

She stepped out and handed Michael a set of 4 black and white photos, her bare back turned toward the lens as she rested her head on her shoulder. She changed her position and facial expression for each shot. In the last one she placed her hand on her shoulder and rested her head on her knuckles. She closed her eyes as if she was dreaming, or deep in thought.

"These are great."

"Want to get another drink?"

"Depends on what you want to talk about."

"Oh, I forgot. Right. My idea for the project."

She reached into her bag and removed her journal. Tom Waits' gritty voice rumbled through the overhead speakers like waves crashing against the shore. She laid the book out flat on the bar and pressed down on the binding. The pages were numbered to correlate to the 8 phases of the moon. Each drawing showed waves slamming themselves onto the beach, spilling water over the sand. On the first page she'd written *new moon*. A figure stood naked and barefoot on the sand in almost complete darkness looking out at a great expanse of sea.

"I love that we barely see you, but feel the strong presence of your form."

Michelle flipped to the next page and revealed the tops of white sea caps rolling toward the figure. She wore a long open sweater. A small section of her face and breasts were lit, echoing the curve and glow of a waxing crescent. Her hips leaned to one side as her arms reached upward as if trying to hold the entire black sky, a portrait of strength and light in the face of mystery.

"These are great."

"Thanks, I thought so, too. There's more."

"All eight phases?"

She put her lips to the glass.

"Not quite."

"You haven't worked it all out yet," he said, tilting his head and furrowing his brow.

She brought the glass to her lips and let the last drop slide back into her throat.

"Sort of, but there's a lot I just have to do by feel. I'll know when I get there," she said, carefully centering the base of the wine glass in the middle of the round coaster.

"You want to talk about it?"

She reached across the bar and pulled the candle jar closer.

"Tonight is an interesting phase, I don't know yet how it fits."

"Which is it?"

She adjusted her body so she'd be at eye level with the jar resting on an upper bar counter, closed one eye and looked straight into the glow.

"The waning gibbous."

***

The waves washed over her feet as she sank deeper into the sand.

A tiny piper skipped over the foam, picking the meat from a rolling sand crab. She closed her eyes and balanced on one leg. The roar of the sea was deafening. She sensed a presence creeping toward her and soon felt a hand land gently on her shoulder, confirming her intuition. A large wave crashed nearby, spreading water between her ankles.

"Can you see it," she said, feeling lips press against the nape of her neck.

She opened her eyes and looked over the broad expanse of sea. A seabird rose from the sand, bursting into open water as a sliver of sun appeared on the horizon. She walked slowly into the water. A wave came, knocking her down. Before the next wave came, she pushed down on the shifting sand, propelling her body toward shore. She looked up at the brightening sky and fading moon, straightened her body and quickly leapt over the white foam before the tide could pull her back under.

***

"You almost done?" Danny said, stretching his neck to look over Michelle's shoulder. "We have that meeting with the new group in an hour."

She felt his breath near her neck and pulled away.

"Did you get an answer from your friend at the gallery?"

"I told him you're working with the photographer, Asbury Mike."

"His name is Michael."

She turned the screen toward him.

"Masterpiece," he said, leaning towards her. "Is that a new tat?"

She pulled up her sweater to cover her shoulders.

"Can I see it?"

She looked over at her corkboard where the black and white photos she took in the booth the night before were pinned. She remembered meeting his hand on her shoulder. The way the seabird balanced effortlessly on the wind. The moon as it faded into the changing light of the day. The way she rose up out of the water before it could pull her under.

"Sure."

She bundled her hair and swiveled her chair so her back was toward him.

"What do you think?"

He pulled down on her sweater to expose the entire design.

"I mean, sure, but I don't really get it."

She released her hair and let it fall over the tattoo.

"You still want to have a drink with me after work?" she said.

"Definitely."

"I'll meet you but I first want a commitment from your friend to exhibit Michael's work."

He straightened his back and crossed his arms.

"What do I get for this," he said.

"I'll show you the rest of my tattoos."

***

Michelle woke early to upload all eight sketches with the corresponding notes. She arranged them in order from the new moon to the waning crescent. Each musing was accompanied by a photo from NASA and showed the moon's surface as it rotated around Earth.

"Got your email," Michael texted.

"What do you think?"

Just as she would be staring at the hypnotic rhythm of white caps as a full moon spread its pull and glow over the ocean, she watched the undulating dots move across her screen and lost herself for a moment, felt herself drift away.

"These are amazing!!!"

She closed her eyes as she swallowed the bitter taste of the night before, with Danny. Michelle punched in Michael's cell number and waited to hear his voice.

"You think so?" she said.

"Send me your schedule for the next two weeks so we can plan to shoot."

"I have vacation time coming up at the end of the month. I can stay with my friend in the city so I don't have to go back and forth."

At the far end of her desk was a shadow box frame. Michelle painted a detailed scene of waves crashing against a rock as a seabird flew overhead. In between the rock and the open sky she pasted the black and white photo of her back she took in the booth. She attached a tiny vintage-style magnifying glass over the tattoo to enlarge it so the viewer could see it clearly, to indicate what was important. The seabird appeared to be craning its neck as it looked down at the detailed winter branch and phases of the moon.

"I have a little gift I made for you. Could we meet at the bar this week?"

There was a long silence.

"Hello, you still there?"

"I have another meeting with the folks at OMAN Gallery to hopefully finalize an exhibit there."

"Great. Did you discuss the idea at your first meeting?"

"Yes but they didn't say much about it. They just listened politely and kept looking at each other."

She glanced at the full moon sketch on her screen.

"Maybe they're mulling it."

"I hope so. Let's meet tomorrow and we can lay out the whole thing so I have the visuals locked in."

"Sure, and I'll bring the little present I made."

"Oh right, that too," he texted. "I'm really excited about this project. Thanks, Michelle."

***

They sat in the back at a large table along the wall. Michael spread out his computer and Michelle took notes as they detailed each of the 8 shoots.

"We are truly on to something," he said, smiling.

"We are."

He raised his hand and spread out his fingers. She wanted to squeeze his fingers and press them to her cheek.

"Let's celebrate with a glass of champagne."

"Yes," she said, responding with a high five.

She followed his steps as he disappeared into the crowd at the bar. A light flashed from her cell screen. It was a text from Danny.

"My friend said he'll do it. He said you can sign the contract. I'll get some weed on my way over. We'll celebrate."

She turned her phone screen-down and slid it away from her. Michael placed the narrow glass in her hands.

"Cheers to us."

They clinked their glasses together. He opened his arms to give space for her to enter. She leaned in and turned her head to glance through the open windows at the moon.

"It's getting late," she said, pulling back from his advances.

"I'm sorry. I am just so excited."

Michelle flopped down in her chair and opened her backpack.

"This is for you."

As he carefully removed the wrapping, she wished his fingers were touching her shoulders.

"I am intrigued."

Like the moon's many faces from night to night and day to day, she watched his expressions change as the flickering candle danced across his features. An ashen glow appeared as he looked into the box; the old Moon in the new Moon's arms.

"This is crazy beautiful," he said.

As if in a trance, Michelle reached back behind her head and pulled out a French hair pin.

"Let me walk you home."

A mass of hair fell over her bare shoulder but the knot remained closed. She pressed her lips against each other and squinted her eyes as she glanced at a waitress turning a metal pole. The awning folded into multiple layers as the moon disappeared behind thickening clouds. She plunged her hand into the knot.

"I'm fine. I'll see you Monday in the studio."

She removed her shawl from behind her chair and wrapped it around her hair and shoulders. Pushing one hand down on the table, she angled herself toward him and pressed her lips against his cheek. A fringe from the shawl dangled over the lit candle, casting shadows against the wall behind them. In the distance, the dark sea churned, spreading white foam over the porous sand. A noisy seabird balanced in the wind.

***

"Can you talk?" Michael texted.

"Sure. Let me find a place to pull over."

"Did you get my email last night?" Michael said.

"No. I was out and didn't open my computer when I got home."

"Well guess what? The fucking OMAN Gallery turned us down. Can you believe it?"

Michelle opened her car window for fresh air.

"Shit. I'm so sorry, Michael."

"Sorry for me? I'm sorry for us! We worked so hard for this."

Her eyes welled up as she remained speechless. A car pulled up behind her. She watched through the mirror as a man with a phone to his ear talked animatedly. He lowered his window and looked up at the morning sky. The moon had disappeared.

"This is so fucked," he said. "All the work is beautiful. I don't understand."

The person in the car seemed to move his left hand in sync with Michael's words.

"You with me, Michelle?"

"Uh, yea, of course I am."

"What d'you think about this? What should we do?"

She remained silent as she steered her car back onto the busy street.

"Where are you, Michael? Are you driving to the train?"

The car behind her also steered off the shoulder and back onto the road.

"Michael. Where are you?"

"Yes. I'm heading to the train. Why do you ask?"

She remained in the right lane and slowed down to under the speed limit to see if the car passed her.

"Just curious as to where you are now."

"I was sure it was a go," he said.

She slowed down to get a better look. But before she could get full recognition the person in the car had closed their dark tinted window.

After working with Michael for a year, she realized she didn't know what kind of car he drove. She didn't know if he had children, if he was in love with someone else and having an affair. She shared the photos of the moon exhibit with her mother and with Danny. He told her the gallery owner needed samples. Who was this gallery owner? she thought to herself. She slammed on her brakes as the car sped up. She craned her neck to look at the license plate. On the back of the car was a bumper sticker of the album cover of Pink Floyd's, *Dark Side of the Moon*. Her memory flashed back to the jogger. Now she remembered. The tattoo he had inked was the same image from the album cover. She remembered how the jogger motioned to her as she sat in the Great Hall. At the other end of the bumper was a sticker that read Asbury51. The name of the gallery of Danny's friend.

***

She threw her keys on her desk and quickly called him back.

"The owner of Asbury51 said he'll give us anything we need."

She glanced down at a note on her desk: See Me When You Get In, Danny

"It's fucking Asbury Park."

"I understand it's not exactly what you wanted, but we can set it up how we envisioned it."

She opened her backpack and pulled out her journal.

"I've just sent over some ideas for promo cards. Tell me what you think."

"No one of any relevance in the art world will trek out there."

She sat down in her chair and put in her ear buds.

"We can set it up exactly how we want and take photos. I'll put the photos together in a presentation and send them to other Chelsea galleries."

Danny entered the room and snuck up from behind. His mass blocked the light from her large computer screen.

"Morning," he said, twisting his body between her and the light of the computer screen.

"Not now," she said, removing one of the buds from her ear. "I'm on the phone."

He dropped a contract from the gallery on her desk.

"A client, I hope?"

"Hey, I'll text you in a minute."

She turned to see if Danny had left the room and googled the OMAN Gallery. On their calendar under October was written, Self Portraits With Moon Glow: Anatomy of our Phases, by Dara Owings.

"We have our dates for Asbury51," she texted. "They're giving us 2 months instead of 1. I'll oversee the design work. It will be great. No, it will be transformational for both of us."

Attached to the bottom of the contract where Michelle's signature was required, a post-it note was attached that read, "you owe me."

"How about we stop by the gallery tonight to check on dimensions. We can have a drink on the beach and go over dates for hanging the photos. It's a full moon tonight."

"I'm not feeling it. Besides, I think I have plans with my wife, Bev."

It was the first time he had mentioned her by name. Michelle coiled a lock of her hair around her finger, pulling it in a taut circle.

"Right, of course."

"Did you ever speak to Dara?" he said.

"About what?"

"Our show. Our ideas?"

"What are you talking about?"

"Look at the damn website," Michael said. "It's about the moon and how the phases affect us humans. Sound familiar?"

"Oh my God."

"How'd she know, Michelle?"

"I didn't say anything. I swear."

"She gave you her card. Did you call her?" he said.

"I thought about it. Just to see if she needed another model. I like her work. But I didn't call in the end. It was a waxing gibbous."

"What? I can't hear you. You broke up."

"I never called her. Believe me."

"What're the chances?"

"Well, the moon is a big fucking object in the vast sky. You're both artists, great artists. So maybe you both fucking looked up one night and saw this big, beautiful glow and you were both, I don't know, hypnotized by it. Artists can be inspired by the same muse, no?"

Michael hung up. She took down her copy of the print from the photo booth, ripped it into pieces and threw it into the trash.

The Studio

Last year they brought an old tugboat to the surface, refurbished it, and turned it into a bar. The inside is solid wood with heavy beams coated with multiple layers of antique white paint. A huge wooden figurehead hangs from the ceiling. Her chest arches over us, her dark eyes wide and mysterious.

The effect of all of this is impressive. The bartender pours me a merlot and fills a bowl with salted peanuts. He asks how I'm doing, and before I can answer, he's screwing a bolt on the underside of an old brass cash register.

These days I find it hard to relax at home. My daughter starts college in the fall and only speaks to me when she's in need of money. My wife nags me all the time about a cottage we saw upstate about three years ago. It's in the mountains. The back deck overlooks a huge lake. A slow-moving stream runs through the front yard and occasionally floods the basement. It's been on the market for some time because no one wants to deal with fixing the crack in the foundation. My wife wants to buy it. I can't find it in myself to understand. She says we can figure out a way to repair it and redirect the water. It's affordable because of the work one would need to put into it, but I have no interest in putting our money into something that's not rock solid. Each time she brings it up, I remind her I'm not good with my hands, and even if I was, we don't have the right tools to fix something that serious. She folds her arms across her chest, squints, and shakes her head. I know it's about more than the cottage. I am losing energy to try to intuit a way forward through this conversation.

I take my wine and peanuts to an empty table near an old copper light. A waitress asks if I want to see a menu. She's petite with cropped auburn hair, freckles, and a tiny glinting stud in her nose. I look up from my fog and swallow. My words stick. I don't know where they went.

"Cat got your tongue?" she asks.

"I'm good for now."

She puts one hand on her hip, tilts her head, and studies my face.

"I usually don't do this," she says, "but I'm in the middle of a photo essay and in need of a subject. All the working models lately are students, but I need an adult, you know? I'm shooting tomorrow at my studio. If you're interested, come by, and we'll see how it goes."

She writes her address on the back of the bill and leaves it on the table.

"And if you regain the ability to speak and want to order something, just give me a shout. My name's Jessie."

The next day I call my wife from work. I tell her I'm going to the bar for a drink before coming home. I walk, feeling the ground under my feet. The studio is in an old warehouse across from the docks. The door is a solid piece of wood with a heavy iron latch. Small track lights hang from rough-hewn beams and run the length of the ceiling. The lights are adjusted to illuminate her photos, which hang from the exposed brick walls. They're striking. And now, seeing the way she's composed them, seeing what she's trying to get at, I'm excited to see what she can do with me in her frame.

"These are yours?"

"Yep. Shot and developed myself."

"They're nice."

The subjects are all burly, middle-aged men. Her manipulation of light spreads a subtle glow over their faces and curates a sense of calm. All the subjects are sitting in an old wood chair pushed against the wall of her studio. I glance around and spot it. Maybe waiting for me. On the floor, next to her camera, is a haunting black and white photo of an elderly sea captain with a dog seated at the prow of a small boat. The subject appears to be in mid-sentence, leaning forward and gesturing into the air.

"Is this also yours?"

"Yep, it's my dad. That's the last photo I took of him before he died."

"It's a nice boat."

"Our neighbors got divorced and split up everything. No one wanted the old boat, so I took it. I found a how-to book in an old nautical shop and refurbished it myself. We loved being out on the water together."

She turns her head and lifts the camera. A flash of light bounces off the stud in her nose. I think about this, what makes a person decide to pierce themselves. Is it a hunger to feel something? A perpetual reminder of pain? I don't ask her, I just sit, and try to pose how she asks, wondering what she's seeing as she shoots.

When I arrive home, dinner is on the table, surrendering its heat to time. I open a bottle of red wine and fill our glasses.

"Didn't you have wine at the bar?" my wife says.

I reach into my backpack and reveal the how-to book. "Yes. This is for you."

She squints and runs her hand over the glossy cover. I watch her smile and realize suddenly it's been a long time since I've caught her off guard in this way. She thinks she knows what to expect from me. How long has it been like this?

"How 'bout we skip the news tonight and snuggle up with our new book?" I say.

"Sure," she says. Then a new idea comes into her eyes. "If we buy the house, do you think we can turn the room with the view of the lake into an art studio? I've been missing my sculpting. What do you think?"

"I think it's a great idea."

That night, I lay awake listening to rain fall on the roof. I remove the book from my wife's chest and place it on her nightstand. In the distance, there is a crack of thunder. A burst of wind pushes through the open window, through the screen, separating the delicate lace curtains.

I wonder why she hasn't pressed me about where the book came from.

Little Death

Each night our mascot—a black and white cat—sneaks into the base searching for a warm lap and scraps of food. Tonight our experienced reconnaissance unit joins an elite group of young, combat infantry soldiers. These scrappy soldiers volunteer for their unit with the promise of death missions into enemy territory. I wonder why the cat isn't afraid of these men, their lack of fear, so thick it sets me on edge. Our orders are to confiscate cars and drivers' licenses from local farmers. This allows us to drive through villages undetected and gather information about terrorist activity. I know what hasn't been said. I know these young guys in my ranks feel untethered, buzzing with adrenaline at the implicit license to do whatever it takes.

"Be careful tonight," our captain warns. "When you get back there'll be hot chocolate on the stove."

Darkness falls. We set ourselves into ambush formation and wait for our prey. I sometimes think I was crazy to sign on for this.

"Get out of the car and hand me your license," the infantry commander barks.

"By whose authority," the farmer says.

"Fuck you—that's whose authority."

The farmer slowly gets out of his car and looks into the commander's eyes.

"If I give you my car I can't get to work, if I can't get to work I lose my job, if I lose my job I can't feed my family—no, I can't give you my car."

The commander waits for him to finish and then cocks his gun and points it at the ground.

"If you don't give us your car you lose your foot," he says.

The farmer looks at the ground where the commander is pointing the rifle and says, "I can't give you my car."

Suddenly there is a rustle in the bushes and the little cat appears, a flash of black and white. For a moment his meow breaks the tension and there's nervous laughter from everyone—except the farmer and the commander, locked in a staring contest.

"Let's return his license and move on," I say.

He looks at me as if I am less than a soldier—but agrees. He gives the farmer his license and slams the butt of his rifle into his stomach. The farmer doubles over and falls to his knees.

We return to the base before dawn, sip hot chocolate and sit around recounting the mission. Suddenly there's a noise in the nearby woods—the commander tells everyone to get down and be quiet. Our mascot comes prancing into our party, rubbing his body against the commander's leg. We all break out in laughter. He looks at me with a forced smile, cocks his rifle and with one shot silences the cat forever.

Somehow I knew this would happen. I knew the cat's lack of fear was strange.

I panic at the thought of what else I know.

Unknown Author

I will always return the books you lend me because I know they are important and remember you told me you are a collector of fine things and

in your bedroom there is a shelf where you have a collection of books in alphabetical order and sometimes you stare at the shelf when you are alone which happens more often now than you prefer but still you feel protected and rich not in the bank or investment portfolio type of wealth but rather the supply and demand type where others might want to steal what you have if they knew what these books meant to you

but they don't know and you have them.

With me you seem to take pity, saddened at my tattered heart and invite me in and serve me fruit and watch how quickly I devour even the pits which are bitter and hard and say you have something that just might be the right thing for me at this time and go to your bedroom shelf pull out a rare book you found years ago at a garage sale upstate in a town that used to be thriving with a main artery flowing with stores and cafes until one day the factory that manufactured intricate embroideries closed down as the price to make them abroad under dark circumstances became cheaper and purchased it for a dollar from the owner who told you he lived through it all lost everything including his wife

who could not be cured from a rare disease of the heart when the town

started to decay her friends moved out and he began to write books and detach from reality sink deeper into a world of fiction with mansions and parties and gilded dreams she could not understand and one day she broke and he gathered all his beloved books then made a sign that read

rare books by unknown author

and stuck it in the hallowed ground where she once gardened and he looked at you with your hand-sewn white dress and recommended a rare book by unknown author who never used proper grammar or clear diction or the right punctuation and you told all this

to me as your cat remained transfixed on my eyes making me

a little uneasy and I finished the last strawberry and you said that each time you pulled this rare book from your sturdy shelf you needed to sit down on your couch because the words like minor chords made your knees weak and when you were deep into the book by the unknown author you wouldn't eat for days or answer texts from friends because you had all you needed and even though you read the book numerous times the arc of the story near the end still leaves you with a sense of melancholy when the man on the bridge gives his hand to the woman with the simple white dress who is thinking about the end.

Syncopated Rhythms

At the end of each song he lays the saxophone on his lap, leans over and spits into a tin bucket. The floorboards under his chair are worn from years of so many sets of heels tapping syncopated rhythms all anchored to this same spot. His toe breaks through the sole of the boot, yet the shine remains jet black and sharp. Droplets of blood attach to his saliva like red delta mud after a storm. He knows, but his face stays stoic—skin stretched tight accentuating his angular features. His back stays straight as he bends over the bucket to look.

The herd of tourists clap then quickly head for the exit; soon another group replaces them. He shifts his weight and slowly turns to his bass player and drummer, and in a raspy voice says, "'Round Midnight in E flat." As he settles into the melody his blood and breath combine to form notes emanating from his gut spiraling into the atmosphere we share. Swirling melodic riffs that grab at the fibers of my soul, filling it.

After his solo he spits again. A small stream of blood remains on his upper lip and hangs there. He wipes it with the back of his hand and flings it down. The saliva lands on his boot; his eyes connect with mine. With a trembling hand he lifts his whiskey flask to his lips, takes a swig and winces. My cell phone vibrates. "Dad, how are you? Great news! I just got word from The New England Conservatory and they're offering me a full scholarship. You'll need to rent a white tuxedo and bow tie for parent's week."

I close my eyes and wait for the music to begin again.

On The Eighth Day

I made a promise to leave my journal in the cabin during the day. This small act would give me pause from writing down every thought entering my head. I could be present within my surroundings, enjoy the mountains. If ideas popped into my head, I'd have no choice but to remember them. This would help to broaden the arc without getting lost in small details. My new work was to revolve around a woman who'd live alone in a small cabin on the banks of the Columbia River Gorge. She'd work for an alternative-energy company. Their motto: *Keep Your House Polar by Using Solar*. She'd go door to door. One day, she'd pull into a driveway and park next to a man idling in an expensive sports car.

"Are you the owner?" she'd say.

"No, just renting for the week."

She'd ask if she could drop off an information packet. The guy would glance at the material and say something like, "In theory, you're on the right track, and I'm with you. I know you're doing important work."

"But…."

"It's too expensive. The locals here will never buy it. Are you from around here?"

They'll bump into each other again at a weekly farmers' market. He'll pull in with his Porsche—yes, that's it, a 911—she on her bike. There'll be a wine tasting hosted by a new organic vineyard. She'll sip more wine than she probably should, then purchase more than she can comfortably fit into her saddlebags.

More, always wanting more.

My man with the Porsche will pull up next to her and watch, amused, as she's engrossed in her attempt to make all the bottles fit.

"It looks like you got more than you can carry."

It will take her a moment to place him, but then she'll remember. Memories aren't so different from wine bottles. They require storage. They take up space.

"25 percent off regular retail price."

I'll figure something to put in here to allow pause and let the reader soak up the symbolism. I want this moment to embody a pure unspoken connection. I want these two people to stand in for anyone who's ever yearned toward something they don't understand.

Then my guy will say something like, "I'd be happy to drive you to your house then bring you back to get your bike."

My hope is to set this kind of backdrop for my growing list of suburban readers. Unhappy with all he has, Romeo meets Grateful Dead Hippie Chick. A turning green love affair.

On the surface, anyway. I'm searching now, trying to find my way deeper, to figure out what this story wants, what it means. I'm convinced I can maintain commercial success with my art, that these are not contradictory impulses.

As I climb to a lookout for a view of the western slopes, I think of friends, colleagues I can approach to read a draft and post comments on my site. I recall the buzz after Book Blondie reviewed my last book. I spent a small fortune wining and dining her, but it was worth it, just as she promised. Just as my wife promised, too. She was thrilled at this new channel opening for me, for us. It took the sting out of our new consciousness of the need to pay for our son's college tuition.

"It's all about what the reader wants," my editor says. "Think of your book like an item on a menu. What will entice the person to order it?"

At first, I resisted.

"I'll follow my own path," I told her.

"You were following your own path before you met me, weren't you?"

She had a point, I conceded.

And after making the best-selling list and watching sales tick heavenward, I never looked back. Whatever advice she gave me, I followed. These days, the only life or death question I ask myself is, How do I sustain it? What do my readers want? With my expenses mounting, I have to find the right story to sell to my patrons, then another, then the next. It never stops.

I find myself here, in the mountains, because I need to find my next novel, yes, and also peace. On my way down the slope and back to the cabin, I piece together the last scene. I can imagine being asked at my book launch, "How did you come up with that ending about Mikey switching his 911 for an electric vehicle? I didn't think he'd ever give up his pride and joy for her."

"Remember she was on the *Going Green's* '50 Sexiest Environmentalists.' I think you'd probably do the same."

I can speak their language.

I shower and have dinner at the picnic table under a thatch of beautiful tall cedars. With only one day left before I head home, I'm anxious to jot down the notes for the last chapter. I gather my leather journal and settle into my camping chair. My hand moves in quick, powerful bursts. The page fills quickly with ideas about Mikey's decision as I work toward tension. I'm always amazed at how my stories evolve from a seed of a simple idea to a full-formed novel. My readers tell me it feels like it's happening to them. They can totally relate to the reality of my characters.

And I can totally relate to them. I sometimes feel a loneliness in this, that these people see my stories, but they don't see me, don't see what it takes to build them, how sometimes it's a stumble through the dark.

"Love how you crafted this story to be like a continuation of the last one," they might say.

"It is so clever. How do you come up with this?" one will ask.

"Keep it real," my editor says. "Stick to things your readers see every day. That's the recipe."

"Way to go," says my wife, her smile newly radiant, her perpetual worry eased by the money my writing puts in our pockets.

I hear something in the distance. I turn my head and catch a glimpse of a woman deeper in the woods, patches of fabric I understand to be her clothes hanging on surrounding branches, her skin illuminated, glowing by the light of the moon. She is naked and completely still. It takes me a moment to understand that she looks to be meditating. A surge runs through my body as a gentle wind plays on my face. I strain to stay awake. I sense my fist open. The pen rolls over the journal. I anticipate a light thud as it falls in the leaves at my feet. The hoot of a nearby screech owl grows desperate. My head rolls back. My eyes close. I feel a warm breath on my face. I disconnect and float into the night's ether.

I'm jolted awake by a crash. My body feels heavy in the folding chair. I shake my head to try to make sense of what is happening. A few feet from my chair, a large shadow stands on its hind legs, licking the remains of my dinner on the table. It snorts and grunts continuously before dropping the plate, scanning around for something else to consume. I am frozen with fear. My first thought is to throw something to distract him. I remember reading that you should make noise when hiking so that bears know you're coming. Black bears have no interest in humans unless we can offer them something to eat. I pick up the leather journal from my lap and heave it. It lands in the dense woods about 20 feet from the table. The bear freezes and turns its massive snout in the direction of the noise. My blood thunders as he lumbers past me. Panicked by what might happen next, I hold my breath and wait. I think of my wife getting the phone call, my son's thin arms wrapped around her. I think of my wife before all of this, when life was less complicated by financial needs. I remember my wife and son when he was newly born, the glory of him and of what my wife and I had made together, his presence something inexorably true, and, in this way, like the purest form of art.

The hoot of the screech owl returns. Confident the bear is gone, I get up slowly and walk to the edge of the woods. With only the light from the moon illuminating the ground, I notice pieces of the pages scattered everywhere. Hundreds of tiny strips lay across the forest bed. I lift one up and hold it close to my face, where I can smell the bear, an enveloping, animal scent. Each strip is like a concertina accordion. The white paper is brown from the bear's paws. My writing is indecipherable. I bend down into thick ferns and reach for what was my journal's leather cover. Staring at what the bear has made of my writing, I am in shock. A week's worth of work is unrecoverable, the story I came here to write.

Before entering the cabin, I turn to take one more look at the carnage. I cringe when I think of my novel in the bear's mouth. Thick drool blotting out pen marks as its teeth tear through the outline and opening paragraph of Chapter One. A woman content with her community of like-minded environmentalists struggles each month to meet rent and keep her cabin with the sweeping views of the river gorge. The man who can take as many vacations as he desires and go anywhere in the world is unhappy. All my labor from the past seven days, meticulously detailing their lives and all their discontent, has been torn to shreds.

As I open the screen door, I notice a figure on the porch of the adjacent cabin. It's through the woods about 20 yards away, so it's difficult to make out the details. I step gingerly off my porch and position myself for a better view. I see the bear lumbering up the stone steps to the raised platform. The person sitting in the chair appears to be a woman, the woman I saw before, dressed now in a simple shift dress. I step closer to confirm my thoughts. I don't understand what my eyes are attempting to pass along to my brain. It can't be true. It must be my imagination, and yet, when I blink, here is the image again, insisting on the truth of itself, and still, I can't believe it. The woman holds out her hand, palm up, in the direction of the bear's nose. Like making contact with a small puppy, the woman seems to wait for the wet touch of the animal's nose. The bear licks her hand, then seems to lower its head, and they stay still that way for a long time. Eventually, the woman resets her glasses onto her face and returns to her book, which seems to signal to the bear that now it's time to go. It turns its massive body, steps down from the porch platform, then disappears into the night.

I pinch the skin on my forearm. Pain runs through the nerves and registers in my brain.

Shaken, I awake early. I'd lain unable to sleep for hours, remembering the improbability of what I'd seen the night before, questioning my grip on sanity. As I light the camping stove to boil water, I piece together fragments of the vision of the woman and the bear. I gather my hiking boots and step outside. Raindrops from a late-night storm linger like silver pellets on fern leaves. The air is thick and sweet. I spread open my topographic map and plan my route. The elevation lines of Big Moose close like an accordion as the trail loops to the top. Confident I'll be rewarded with sweeping views from the mountaintop, I check to see how many exposures remain in my old camera. In this age of rapid-fire cell phone photos, film limits me to only 24. I bring only one roll so each shot is precious. I've trained myself to view landscapes with a discerning eye. I look inside the tiny window. It indicates I have two exposures remaining.

So precious. Just two. I have to make them count.

I turn my head in the direction of the cabin where I saw the woman and the bear, and I wonder why I didn't reach then for my camera. I'd been frozen, trying to understand this thing unfolding before me. As a fiction writer, I've learned the art of twisting truths to enhance the story. Leave your readers thinking that you might have experienced this, or that you really wanted that car. I know that my editor will rent the Porsche 911 for me to drive up to my book launch. I just play into it. It's a living, a good one. I'm lucky, I remind myself. I wanted this, and now I have it.

I do the dishes before heading out. I figure I'll stop by the office on my way to the trailhead. I want to find a way to ask if they've heard reports before of strange bear sightings. I have to ask, I tell myself.

I lock the cabin door and walk back to the table. I stuff the map into the outer pocket of my backpack and look around for my camera, which isn't where I left it. There's an unmistakable rustling sound in the woods directly beyond my folding chair. My camera dangles from the back of the chair, swaying like a metronome. Goosebumps prickle over my skin, and, again, for the second time in less than a day, I'm frozen in fear. Fresh footprints have appeared in the dirt. Two have what look like sneaker treads. The other two look like, yes, bear tracks. They appear side by side and go past the chair and into woods so dense I won't follow.

I can hardly form a sentence in my mind, much less think how to push it out of my mouth, to coax it from my pen. I don't trust what seems real. I don't understand anything.

***

The ascent to the summit is more challenging than the contour lines on the map indicated. After three hours, the trees dwarf and the long ridge opens up to a spectacular view. To the west, the high peaks rise up like walls of snow-capped curtains against a bright blue sky. To the east, a huge lake shimmers as the sun's rays dance across it. The wind above the tree line is relentless. I remove my sweat-drenched shirt and put on a fresh fleece. I lay down my backpack, remove my binoculars, and lean my back against a large boulder. In the distance along the adjoining ridgeline, a person moves quickly along the trail. It appears to be a woman with a large black dog. I think it looks like the woman in the woods, but who knows if I'd think this about any woman now, anywhere. Isn't this a function of post-traumatic stress? The mind plays tricks.

The woman and creature ascend at a fast clip. Suddenly, the light shifts as thin clouds pass in front of the bright sun. Vivid beams break through an opening and move along the valley floor. I take out my camera, press the viewfinder against my eye, and press down on the button. There is no resistance. The film advance lever will not move. It indicates I've come to the end of my 24 exposures, even as I know I had two left when I set out. I know I did, I'm sure of it.

I rewind the film, then drop it into the plastic film canister. The footsteps of the hiker grow louder as they get closer to where I sit. I try to imagine a faithful dog barreling through the low trees in order to shake this foreboding sense that it's the woman and the bear, which can't be true.

The hiker passes in front of me. Etiquette dictates that I should nod and say something like, "Amazing view," but the figure ignores me completely, looks straight ahead, and keeps walking. It's her. It's absolutely her. This is not my mind playing tricks on me; it's her, the naked woman, the woman with the bear, right in front of me. She has long black hair, a faded jean jacket, and the loose-fitting dress she wore last night as I watched her. A wave of anger passes through me. Why, I can't say. I'm tired of feeling unsettled, tired of feeling at a loss to explain what's around me.

"I'm here," I say under my breath, moving my head back and forth knowing she can't hear me. "...and where's your big black dog?"

I find her lack of acknowledgment rude. I can imagine her strolling into her day job. Let's say she's a computer analyst. She looks straight ahead, coffee in hand, and doesn't say a word to her coworkers. At the end of the day, she gathers her stuff and walks out. Head in the clouds.

"Not even a nod to the security person in the front lobby."

She stops in her tracks and stands like that for a few moments. I watch the back of her head, her black hair glossy in the sunlight.

"Are you talking about me?" she says, turning her head to look at me.

Astonished by her unexpected response, I quickly whip my head up and gather her into focus.

"What?"

"You heard me."

I wonder if she saw the movement of my head teasing her when she walked by.

"No, no, of course not. Just talking to myself. It's a beautiful view from up here."

I hear movement on the rocks behind me. The bear. Again, I'm frozen.

"Probably just a bear," she says grinning, and I swear she can see my fear.

She disappears beyond the ridge, and I sit for a long time listening to the woods around me.

On my way down, the sky opens up. Rain and awful hail make the descent difficult, even treacherous. The creeks, which were almost dry when I started the ascent, are now gorged with swift-moving water. The fresh mud from the banks mixes with the white caps and washes downstream, whirling in violent patterns. In order to continue my descent and not veer away from the trail, I'd have to cross the raging waters. I position myself on a large rock and watch the angry water. I feel light-headed and tired. My legs shake as I ponder the jump. I bend my knees and leap. I land on my target, but the rock is slippery. I feel the weight of my body fall backward and, with a thud, land in the freezing water. The angry current pushes me downstream. I reach out in desperation and grab for a tree root that hangs over the stream. I clutch it with all my might and hold on. The torrents of water feel like continuous punches in my stomach. Rain continues to pour down on my head. My mouth fills with water as I try to elevate my body to higher ground. I am in serious danger of getting swept away, and my only thought is to keep my camera dry. With my strength nearly zapped, the same picture of my wife receiving the call with my son at her side comes rushing back. I close my eyes and, with everything I have left inside, hoist one leg onto the bank. My heel catches a tree root, giving me just enough leverage to grab a branch and swing my body out of the water. I crawl like an animal through the mud to safe ground. I quickly remove my backpack and unzip the pocket. The lens of my camera is filled with water, like the cabin of a sinking ship. I reach my hand deeper into the pack and remove the plastic film canister. I open the top. The finished roll of film I put inside the sealed canister is dry.

Leaning against a tall cedar, I wait for my breath to settle. I look out at the raging river I crawled out from and contemplate my two near-death experiences. The last 24 hours of my self-imposed writing residency should have been a wrap-up and celebration of the outline and first chapter of my next novel. Instead, it has turned into a total disaster. The rain continues to fall in sheets. I look up beyond the dripping branches to the thick gray clouds and close my eyes, feeling the air and water on my face.

Drained and defeated, I duck into the registration office.

"I guess you should've read the reports today," the man behind the counter says. "I posted them at the first light of day."

"Next time I'll be sure to check. You have any spare paper? Last night a bear came into my area and destroyed my journal."

Where before the idea of telling someone about what I'd seen had given me pause, now I found that something had loosened in me, and I no longer cared what anyone thought. The irrational anger I felt toward the woman on the mountain returned now, this time directed at the man before me, who thought it was funny that I'd been out in that fierce storm on the mountain, utterly vulnerable.

"*Your* area?"

I edit the phrase in my head and say, "Yeah. I was sleeping outside in my chair, in the area that I paid for, for the week of my time here, and heard this sound, then I awoke."

"What time was it?" he says as he sinks below the counter. I hear his hands tapping against the thin wood. "I know it's here somewhere."

"Probably after midnight, why? Is there like a curfew against humans being outside after a certain hour?"

After what seems like a long time to find paper, he eventually rises. Like a man holding a trophy fish for a photo opportunity, he straightens his back, blows dust off the top, and hands me a ream of vintage stationery paper.

"It was after midnight? So it was today that you saw the bear?"

"So?"

"You reserved the cabin for seven days."

"That's right. Today is the seventh day."

He looks over my head to the parking lot.

"You need to pack up. We rented it to a couple for this afternoon. They do a lot of smooching. Probably just got married or just met, or they're both married to someone else or something?" he says, closing one eye as if he's revealing a great secret. "They're waiting for the room."

Water drips onto the paper from the brim of my hat.

"He's got that fancy car out there."

I turn my head but cannot see beyond the giant wood carving of a bear.

"I got some plastic you can wrap the paper in."

He slides the stack into a plastic bag.

"Give me a hand, will ya," he says, stretching out a large rubber band. "That should keep it dry till you get back to...your cabin."

"Yeah, thanks. Well, I appreciate this."

"Just some old paper that guests would use to write letters home. Before emails, of course."

He puts his elbows on the counter and leans forward close to my face.

"Funny, cause I was gonna throw 'em out this week."

"Right. Listen, I have a question for you. Do you know the woman in the cabin next to mine?"

There's a prolonged silence.

"Like...in the biblical sense?" he says, straightening his back and folding his arms across his chest. "You accusing me of some after-hours snooping?"

I ignore this insinuation.

"I swear I saw a bear sniffing her hand."

His eyes glance at the bulletin board under the wall clock.

"She's a bit...let's say, different."

"In what way?"

He looks down at his room ledger and stretches his large hand across both temples.

"You a detective?" he says without looking up.

"I told you I'm a writer."

He stands straight up. I watch his chest inflate as he takes in the stale office air.

"She's got quite a story, actually" he says with clenched jaws as he sinks again below the counter.

"Keep this to yourself, Shakespeare," he says.

I watch the top of his head bob back and forth as he looks for something.

"I found it."

He lays down on the counter a yellowed newspaper wrapped in plastic.

"This was a huge deal here. People stopped coming. We nearly had to close down. Folks got freaked out about this. I don't blame 'em, but they forget, this is the wilderness. I forgot the article was here until the other day when I started cleaning up a bit."

He looks at my arms clutching the paper wrapped in plastic.

"Meant to throw it out with the other stuff. Just never got around to it. I guess it's worth holding onto some stuff. You never know."

On the front page is a picture of a woman sitting on a bench clutching her head in both hands. Her long dark hair covers her facial features. She wears a jean jacket and summer dress. It's her.

"This her?"

"Writers don't read anymore?" he says, staring out at the parking lot. "The story's there for you."

Sensing the man will not give me long, I run my eyes quickly across the faded ink. The article is long and detailed. I stand erect and hold the article in my hand at a distance to allow space, like when I take photos of sweeping landscapes. My eyes glance over the story as a whole as each paragraph bleeds into the next. I let the details sink in. The woman comes to a cabin with her young son to celebrate his birthday. They go out hiking. Along the ridge, at Big Moose Trail, they encounter a bear. The young boy is carrying the food in his pack. The bear chases him and slashes at his neck to get at their lunch. The jugular is severed, and the boy dies instantly.

As I read, I forget to breathe. I think of my wife, my son. My wife in my son's arms as he struggles to comfort her. I think of the woman, naked and motionless in the woods, her clothes hung carefully from the branches around her. I think of the bear, its stillness, timidity almost, as it approached her on the porch that night.

"She comes every year at this time," he says. "Guess it's the anniversary of the kid's birthday."

The events from last night rush through me.

"Awful. Thanks for the paper."

I lift my wet pack and head towards the door.

"Still raining," the man says. "You don't want it to get wet. You can sit over there and write. I won't bother you."

The words ricochet off the old panel walls. I put the paper under my shirt and against my skin. I zip up my jacket and turn towards the man at the counter. The old story and the two characters, now in tatters strewn across the earth, seem a bit out of sorts. Perhaps the near-death experience from a bear or almost getting washed away from a raging creek sealed my fate. I'm not sure where this is going, but maybe my self-imposed seven-day writing retreat was only a beginning.

"Do you have any cabins for the coming week?"

My wife will understand, even encourage me to stay until I find what I need.

Like molasses, he slides his index finger over the pencil marks of each reservation.

"The couple will take your cabin, but I can move you to another."

"I think that's what I need."

I listen to the ticking of the wall clock as I wait for him to finish. I think about how she passed me on the ridge. I wonder if the spot where I sat and judged her as she passed was the same place where she and her child sat together for the last time.

"She's checking out today," he says, glancing at the bulge of my jacket. "You can move into her cabin."

"You mean *her*?" I say pointing to where the article lays on the counter.

"Yep," he says, picking up the article.

"That suits me fine."

He opens his grip, letting the paper float into the trash can. I sign the registration form and walk outside. The heavy downpour gives way to intermittent raindrops. Sharp rays of light break through the tall cedars. A middle-aged woman carrying a stack of white towels piled up to her eyes walks in the direction of my cabin.

"I'll be packing up now and heading over to that one."

She rests her chin on the top towel and removes a folded piece of paper from her back pocket.

"The woman gave me this. She wanted me to put it in your cabin."

"You see her today?"

"Yes. She just left a few minutes ago. The way she always does. Through the woods."

In the middle of the note was a taped torn piece from my journal. Underneath appear the words, *toksha ake wacinyuanktin ktelo*.

"Do you know what this means?"

"I think it's Lakota. I'm not Lakotan, but I have an app on my phone."

She places her hands on the top and bottom of the white towels and carefully transfers the pile to me.

"Thank you," she says, removing her phone from her back pocket.

"It means, I'll see you later."

Resting my chin on the top of the pile, I turn the paper over to show her a grouping of three words, *Hu Nunpa Mato*.

"What about this?"

"It says, *Hu Nunpa* means standing up on two legs. *Mato* is the word for the spirit of a bear. There's a link. I can look it up if you're OK with the towels?"

"I'm good."

"*Hu Nunpa Mato* comes from the legend of a great bear who lay asleep, but he was actually listening to the spirits. Mato was quiet and an observer. Mato was well respected. He always remained calm. When it came time to pay respect and sing praise, he stood up on two legs, *Hu Nunpa*. After he sang an honor song for all spirit and energy, Mato was told he would be the protector of all Medicine Men and Holy Men. To this day, he stands on two legs to view what we call the spirit-scape to see who'll remember and welcome his song and his eternal knowledge."

She returns the phone back to her pocket. I transfer the white towels into her open arms, then refold the note and slide it under the rubber bands.

I feel a chill. I remember the bear at my table, eating the remnants of my dinner, then looking for more, eating my work, my words.

***

On the morning of the eighth day, I awake with a renewed sense of purpose. I make coffee, collect my pens and paper, and step outside. Circling above the clearing in the trees, an eagle soars, and I stop to watch. Though I'm only a few hundred feet from the old cabin, it feels a world apart. Something feels different. I think of the firm goals I set for my seven-day, self-imposed residency. I look again to the sky. I rest the ball of the pen on the old stationary paper and inhale the cool, morning air. I can see my characters and the opening scene, but my hand doesn't move. I force out a few words describing the River Gorge and the woman with her fliers. I write the name of the guy with the Porsche, then sip coffee from my tin cup. A shadow from the large bird spreads over the stationary paper. I look up at its wings spread wide. Effortlessly, it climbs higher and higher. Watching this magnificent creature, I retrace the events of the last few days. I cross out the lines about the woman and the Porsche and set the paper aside, making space for something new, allowing it to come to me, embracing and welcoming it here.

During my week-long, self-imposed writing residency, I made a promise to leave my journal in the cabin during my day hikes. This small act gives me pause from writing down every thought that enters my head. I can be present within my surroundings and enjoy the mountain scenery. If ideas for my new novel pop into my head, I have no choice but to remember them. This helps to broaden the arc without getting lost in small details. My new work would revolve around a woman who rents a cabin at the same time each year on the date of her son's tragic death....

"This is *not* what we talked about," my editor will say. "Who's gonna read this?"

I smile to think of it: newly, strangely, freed from care.

Like a black dot against an endless blue sky, the eagle rises to new heights. I shade my eyes and watch as it diminishes before disappearing. I go back inside to find a pillow to sit on. I anticipate a full day of writing. I grab the note and the envelope with the photos I developed at the drugstore. Walking back to the scene of the reckoning, I notice one of the ripped pages from my journal resting atop a fern leaf. I pick it up and try to read the word. Moist from yesterday's downpour and today's morning dew, the blue ink is indecipherable. I roll it into a ball and place it on the ground near the roots of the Maidenhair Fern.

I return to the table and lay the note next to the photos. The last two photos are blurry and hard to make out, but I have my story. I look down at my new lines and say the words, *hu nunpa*, over and over against the silence of the wilderness. I clutch my pen and try to open myself to imagine her story. The pain she must have suffered, must still suffer. I lift the blurry photo of the woman and adjust my reading glasses. Inked on her shoulder blade is an image of what appears to be a bear standing on two legs. Underneath is the word Lakota, then more words I don't recognize. I'll look them up as soon as I'm able.

I bring the other photo close to my face. Four footprints. Two with sneakers and two of a creature. *Mato*, I say to myself, as the ink flows over the fibers like the banks of a creek after a storm.

Diamond Life Master

An idea for the elusive ending of the story I'm writing woke me this morning. My story concerns a bridge player, Mike. He's married to a woman who loves him. He meets another woman, Ellie, as they both take out their trash. She's new to the neighborhood. He knows this before she tells him, because he feels certain he would have remembered her, though in fact, paradoxically, he senses he already knows her, that they're connected somehow.

The point of my story is to figure out how.

An ennui has settled in. Mike is coping with what so many people do, comfortably embedded in long marriages which are yes, comfortable, yet also completely known, worn, charted. He misses mystery. He finds himself craving transience, flux.

Mike is throwing away a mirror his wife has been bothering him to carry out for the trash. It's uncomfortable, awkward to move, and his breath fogs its glass as he hoists it from side to side, trying to keep a good grip.

"You aren't throwing that away, are you?"

Mike looks up. He takes her in. He'll know her name soon, but he doesn't yet. Now, she could be anyone.

"You think I shouldn't?"

"It'd be pretty easy to fix," the woman says, her face partially blocked by a wool cap. She is bundled up well against the cold that wraps itself around their bodies, around everything it encounters. "I'm a set designer for Broadway. I have tools in my apartment. It wouldn't be a problem for me, it would take me two seconds. Besides, I hate to see good things thrown away."

"That's very kind of you to offer."

"Oh hardly. Really, it's nothing."

She smiles at him.

I live up there, the fourth floor," she says, pointing to the building. "My name's Ellie."

"I'm Mike."

He follows the direction of her hand with his eyes.

"On the fourth floor, you said?"

"Yes, right up there, That's my bedroom with the light on."

She continues to point for a moment, then drops her hand to adjust her hat.

He keeps his focus on her face. She switches her weight to the other foot.

Mike feels unsaid things suddenly fill the air even as he's not sure what they are. He feels strangely uneasy. Ellie breaks the new silence in which he knows her name, and she knows his.

"So do you work here in Brighton Beach?"

Mike wants her to know that he's a bridge player with Diamond Life Master ranking. It's the thing of which he's most proud.

"Yes, but I also play bridge, and my club is only a few blocks from here. It's convenient. Otherwise, I'd probably live in Park Slope."

He hadn't planned for all this to slip from his mouth, but it had, and the words sit in the cold air between them.

"I find bridge such a fascinating game. Do you have a ranking?"

"I do, I'm a Diamond Life Master. The American Contract Bridge League bestowed that honor on me last year. Do you play?"

She tilts her head, never breaking contact with his eyes, and there's a new degree of connection. He suppresses a shiver which might come from something else. He can't tell and doesn't try.

"I do play, but not at your level."

She takes off her hat and runs a hand through her hair. A tumble of dark curls which had been hidden now sifts out through her fingers, glinting in the stray lights of the night. She keeps her eyes on him whether talking or listening. He finds himself wanting to look away for a moment of respite from the building intensity, even as he craves it.

"I'm actually looking for a new partner. Would you be interested?"

"Oh wow, I'd love to learn, but I wouldn't want to mess with your ranking. I'm really a beginner."

"No worries about that, I can hold my own and help you get your footing at the same time, if you'd like? We could take it one game at a time."

He means it. He finds himself hoping she'll say yes, hoping she's not only being polite.

Ellie removes a card from her pocket and extends it to him.

"I'd like that a lot. My number's on the back."

"Great. I'll call you on Tuesday. We can meet right here and walk together."

When she reaches for the mirror, he doesn't immediately understand what she's doing, and when it occurs to him that she was reaching for the mirror, not for him, he felt, at the new lightness of his arms, a slight trembling, a sense that she'd opened something rather than taken it away, cleared a path for a new, as of yet unarticulated, unfigured thing.

And the thing that woke me this morning, the thing I now realize about the ending of Mike's story, the missing link, really, is that Mike recognized Ellie. He understood who she was as soon as she pointed out the fourth-floor window to him as her own. He'd seen her some nights before sitting in that windowsill looking out into the night, brushing her hair. He'd watched her and wondered what she was seeing, what she was looking for, what she was thinking.

This changes my story, changes the whole thing, not just the ending. I'm not daunted even as I realize now I'll have to rewrite, reconsider things.

It changes everything. It's the key.

Mike had fumbled for binoculars that night to see Ellie more closely, before he knew her name, to see the look on her face as she brushed her hair, gazing out into the night, and he hadn't had enough time to absorb her features before he heard his wife's key in the lock of their front door. He eased his binoculars back into the drawer and quietly slid it shut, went out to greet his wife, to hear about the movie she'd just seen even as the methodical rhythm of Ellie brushing her hair stayed lodged in his mind, until he met her the following night, until he'd learn her name.

***

"Be careful tonight, honey. The snow could pile up. Please get out before the roads get too rough."

"Don't worry. I will. Don't wait up, okay? I promise I'll be fine."

"Fine, but call me when you leave the club so I know when to expect you."

"I will, I promise."

"Tell Tatyana I say hello."

"I hope she'll be there tonight."

"I still can't believe you guys won the state tournament."

"I know, isn't it something? It was a good night."

"You were good. You've been playing together for so many years."

"We have."

"Not one bit stale."

"No, not yet. But you know things can change."

"Maybe, but not yet. I'm so proud of you. I love you."

"I love you too, sweetheart."

He embraces her before he leaves, brushes his lips against her waiting, upturned cheek. In the moment he closes his eyes against his wife's face, he sees Ellie's curls swathed in the lights of the night around them, liberated from her wool cap, free against the night.

***

He leaves the apartment, closes the door firmly behind him, rides the elevator down to the lobby. He removes the card from his wallet, soft from where he's fingered it in his pocket over the last few days, and he calls her.

"Hey, it's Mike."

"Mike, hi. Oh, it's Tuesday! Bridge! I completely forgot. It's been a crazy week at the shop. I'm so sorry, and I haven't had a chance to get to your beautiful mirror."

Mike evaluates his hand and makes a bid.

"No big deal. I'm actually calling about the bridge game, the mirror can wait. I was just going to throw it away, anyway."

"You'll see. I'll make it good as new. And I'm so sorry I forgot about the game. I just got home. What do you think about the forecast? It's supposed to really come down soon, do you think it's worth risking?"

"It's not too far, and the salt trucks are all out now. I know they already got the sidewalks. I bet we'll be fine."

"You're probably right, and I hate to say no, but I think I'm going to sit this one out. I love being nestled inside when it snows. Could we say maybe for next week?"

Ellie walks into her bedroom, pushes back the curtain and looks out. She notices the movement of a figure in the dark of an apartment across the way.

She likes looking out the window, catching glimpses of people in the midst of living their lives, imagining themselves alone, unnoticed. She has always loved to watch people, it's what pulled her to her work designing sets, so many constructions of places against which examples of human behavior play themselves out. Now, here, in her new apartment, she's enjoying sitting and seeing what she can once night has fallen and people have retreated into the private worlds of their homes, the lit up boxes of their apartments like so many sets before her, alive all at once.

The window she watches now, though, is dark, but not so dark that she can't see someone, a woman, moving inside. Ellie wonders why this woman does not turn on a light.

Mike has not given up on an outcome where Ellie might need support as they walk down the icy sidewalk along Ocean Parkway. Where her curls might fall across his shoulder as she clutches his arm to keep from slipping in the fresh snow. He wants to feel the weight of them.

"You can absolutely count me in for next week. I'm looking forward to it," she says, barely listening to his response as she watches the woman, more clear now, in the window across the way. It's not apparent to Ellie whether or not the woman is dressed. Even though the apartment is dark, Ellie can see the movement of the woman's figure through the space of the room separated from Ellie only by two panes of glass, the air between buildings.

"My usual partner broke her arm. She's gonna be out of the picture for a while."

Mike knows the bluff is controversial but plays it out to see where she'll take it.

"Oh gosh. That's terrible."

It had been a play to arouse a guilt response in her, but it didn't seem to work. There was silence on the other end.

He doesn't understand that the sudden lack of interest on Ellie's part is due not to anything he's said, but in the emergence of something of greater interest to her in the window across from her, in her view, in the woman she's watching who has pressed herself so closely against the glass that her face, recently revealed, is periodically covered by the transient clouds of steam from her breath. If Mike did know this, if he could see what Ellie saw, he might remember his own breath against the mirror his wife had been bothering him to throw away. But he can't. He can't know that Ellie is wondering if the woman is looking at her. He can't know that Ellie is rapt, imagining suddenly that she can feel the warmth of that woman's breath in the same way Mike imagined he could feel the strokes of Ellie's hairbrush as if he'd become the hairbrush itself, himself.

But soon her attention returns, and she finds her voice.

"I'm sorry. Listen, would you like to come over to work through some situations tonight, and next week we can head out for a game? It would give you a chance to see if we're compatible as a team. We wouldn't have to brave the weather."

A couple that lives on the floor above Mike's apartment exits the elevator. He turns toward the front door and looks around as if he's checking the progress of the snowfall. He knows the importance of keeping his head clear of distraction. Now is the time to concentrate on the game.

He has one chance.

Mike is careful not to answer too quickly.

He steps aside and waits for the couple to leave.

"Sure. That can work for me."

He walks out into the night

At the end of Ocean Parkway
a bright star
like a diamond
appears in the sky.

Ellie greets her partner
with a glass
of Bordeaux,

French perfume
swirls
around her.

She lowers the diamond tip
tonearm
onto a spinning record,

a hypnotic
call and response
of clarinet and gypsy
jazz guitar,

fingers and breath
melt into the
warm glow
of the evening.

Her vulnerability
deepens, opens,

he cuts the deck
and deals
contemplating
his opening
bid.

Snowplows
rumbling east to west
cause a temporary
shift in mood,

unexpectedly
the Queen turns
her card
face down
on the edge
of the table,

extends
her hand
and rises.

The King
plays the Queen
like a beginner,

pulls her close,

presses
his lips
on the curve
of her neck,

swaying
to the rhythm.

She places
her hand
strategically
on his back
between
shoulder blades

waltzes
him into
the bedroom

pulls the chain
hanging
from her lamp

signaling
to the onlooker
across the way.

With all her cards
lined up
in the
same suit

The Queen
guides her partner
to the edge of her bed
and removes
his shoes.

Attacking
his lead
with active defense
she bolts the door
with padlock

then opens
the curtain
revealing
her hand
to the woman
across the way
peering through
binoculars
from her bedroom.

Vulnerable and
exposed
the King
lurches for the exit.

The Queen
looks out
across the way

strokes her hair
with a wide
paddle brush

declares
herself
Winner

then slips
between
the sheets

waiting
for the Diamond
Life Master
to beg
for combination.

And just like that, it's clear. My story is told. I understand why I'm here, why I was called to the page, to make my bid at the truth. Mike and Ellie are cast on the page. I close my eyes and see a mirror, feel the warmth of breath on glass. It's me alone in a dark apartment, moving through the space I inhabit, the domain so familiar to me I don't need to switch on light in order to see. It's also me on the outside looking in. I am everywhere, pen in my hand. The tricks resolve themselves behind my closed eyelids. My hand is balanced. I can sleep again, and wait for the next move to come to me.

The Ending

This morning before driving over the suspension bridge that brought me to where you paint, I shaved my head. Not because I needed to, usually that comes every four days when stubble marks distinct lines between skin and new growth. But this morning I felt something different, the need to do something more. Like after a long hot summer when I once slipped my arms through the worn leather jacket I'd purchased at a secondhand store and felt the cool material on my bare arms, a second skin. Turning sideways I look into the ornate full-length mirror which hangs opposite your painting and squint until the photons settle and my fully bald reflection is clarified. I turn again to your painting and wonder.

I remember you told me once how a Buddhist monk goes through his initiation ceremony. He accepts his precepts, then leaves behind his relationship with the material world, casting aside all his earthly possessions. Everything that was is now lost in the past as he looks ahead to his first glimpse of Enlightenment. Only then can he be free. I wonder how that freedom feels.

I step outside to check the weather and fill my lungs with morning air. I close my eyes and breathe. The image of your painting flashes in the dark of my vision. My body is wrapped tightly inside, fascia coming alive as my internal organs awaken and communicate with each other. I hold my breath longer than is natural. The need for air becomes too great to resist and I breathe again. I see it again, the face a blaze of color and feeling. I was there. I remember.

Driving into the bright morning sun I recall the last chapter of a book I read years ago by Leornard Cohen who said a monastery can be a lonely and dark place. He had too much time to think about his flesh and past relationships, all things he missed from the material world. What remained for him was only a few seconds each day to contemplate higher truths and Enlightenment. How he tried to fit together his different layers of understanding, of yearning. I think about yearning.

I pull down the visor to block the light. The churning in my stomach ceases. I speed up in anticipation of seeing your new art and feel my car careen slightly off-center as it scrapes the cement barricade of the bridge's EZ Pass lane. With no concern for the damage, I find a soul music station as the morning sun spreads its golden light over the sparkling sea below. The barricade is behind me now. The music helps.

As I enter the east-bound ramp of the bridge, I remember you telling me that the subject in the painting hanging opposite my ornate mirror was a prostitute you'd met years ago. You'd asked her how she did it, how she kept her feelings safe.

"Listen, my body is used a dozen times in a day. But I forget as soon as they hand me the money and walk out the door. Except once, maybe twice, I remember. I was swept up, and one of them took me by surprise."

You said you'd put down your brush when she said this.

"Once a customer came in just to talk. I asked if he wanted anything else because he'd still have to pay. It was my time, you know."

"No," he said. "Nothing else. Just this."

"I removed his leather jacket and then his shirt. I held him tight against me. We didn't move. I didn't and he didn't, not once. When the hour was up, I walked out with him, to see him to his car. I'd never done that before. He handed me more money and a Post-it note he took from the dusty table at the entrance where the clay Buddha sits with the incense. On it he wrote, 'I love you.'"

You stopped painting when she told you this, you said, just as I sat so still listening to you. I remembered this as I crossed the bridge.

I think of what it means to love.

***

I parked in the only open spot on a dead-end street in front of a pile of broken plastic pipes. On the right side of the street was a string of mom and pop automotive shops. A blaring drone of machines and drills broke the quiet hum of the Brooklyn morning. Alida's art studio was located in an old warehouse building across the street. Directly in front of the broken pipes was a wrecked car. An unhoused person had set up a home there, crafting a sitting area with several repaired lawn chairs and tens of plants. Each one was set inside clay urns and plastic pots and arranged in two neat rows that led from the passenger door of the car.

"Need something?" he said, as I clicked the button on the key to ensure my car was locked.

"No, just admiring your space."

He paused a minute, then returned to watering his potted plants.

"Your fiddle leaf fig is pretty impressive," I said.

He stood up and shaded his eyes from the morning sun.

"I'm impressed you know its name," he said. "People usually don't. And you can call me Tom."

"Nice to meet you. You can call me Mike."

He poured a full bucket of water into the fiddle leaf fig urn.

"I revived this one for a friend," Tom said. "A miracle of sorts."

I gazed up at the six floors of arch top windows stretching the length of the massive building. In many of them were the silhouettes of artists working. Their bowed heads close to the glass were exploiting the morning light. I imagined them deep in their creative processes affixing elements of the material world to memories of their past, shaping and summoning what they wanted to preserve and leaving the rest.

"Looking for someone?" a man asked as he pushed open the industrial metal door with his hip, muscular forearms wrapped tightly around a large cardboard box.

"Yes. Alida."

He twisted his head and looked up at one of the windows as if to find her there.

"You mean Izabelle?"

I was thrown for a moment but remembered she said she sometimes used different names. But I had never heard her referred to as Izabelle.

"She knows you're coming?"

"Yes."

"You a dealer?"

"I have one of her works."

He crossed the street and handed the box to Tom.

"You should buzz her," Tom said, looking inside the box. "Cell phone reception is spotty up there."

He took a few items out from the box and threw the rest over the plastic pipes. I was struck by the contrast between his orderly rows of plants, the tidiness of the little sitting room he'd made, and this carelessness, the trash now all over the pipes.

As I searched for the name Izabelle in the row of names next to the buttons, the large metal door swung open again.

"Hey."

I turned toward the voice and saw Alida standing in front of me. She wore a pale blue jumpsuit with white converse sneakers. Her clothes were covered in paint.

"I was about to buzz you, but I couldn't find your name."

She pointed to one of the labels.

"Right there."

I leaned closer and saw the name was Izabelle.

She looked at me intensely, squinting, and I had the urge to hide.

"You have a cut on your head," she said. "Looks like it's bleeding."

"Here?" I touched the back of my head. I remembered shaving. I also remembered feeling something, but I hadn't checked before I left the house, just kept moving forward.

Alida leaned closer.

"Yeah. It looks kinda deep. It's still bleeding. I have some alcohol and Band-Aids in my studio."

Alida stood back from examining the wound I'd been oblivious to.

"You gotta slow down," she said, putting her hands on her hips. "Be more careful."

I wanted to say something, but had learned through trial and fire to always hold back.

"Was there traffic?"

"Not really."

"Sorry you had to take such a long drive on a Saturday."

"I enjoy the drive. It's quiet in the morning and gives me a pause to do some thinking."

"What did you think about?"

I'd first met Alida at a dance performance the previous year at a small theater in Williamsburg, Brooklyn. She was with her partner, a soft-spoken woman with bright blue eyes. The audience sat at small cocktail tables set around the elevated stage.

"Can I look at that," she'd asked me, pointing to the program on my table.

"They gave me two," I said. "You can have this one."

Her partner's arms were folded as she stared straight ahead.

"I just want to see when our friend is performing."

"Keep it, no worries."

"Thanks. I'm Alida."

She asked if I knew anyone performing. I told her I didn't and was curious about this new theater that had opened just the month before.

"What's your friend's name?" I asked.

"Carissa."

"He meant your friend the dancer, not me," said Carissa, not turning to look at us or join the conversation.

Alida pointed to a name on the program and leaned toward me.

"Her name is Cory," she whispered. "She's incredible. Wait until you see her."

"She just has a crush on her," said Carissa, looking at Alida and rolling her eyes.

"She's just jealous," said Alida.

"I know her," I said. "She is amazing."

Alida's eyes widened and she went completely still.

"What? No. You're kidding?"

I put on my glasses and looked at her photo.

"She went to Juilliard with my daughter."

"Wow. That's crazy. Is your daughter a dancer, too?"

"A violinist. She was a great musician. They did a bunch of performances together. They were getting somewhere really fascinating."

"Why don't you move over to his table," Carissa said.

"She doesn't play anymore?" said Alida.

"She died a few years ago."

There was that awkward, heavy silence I had almost grown used to but not quite.

"I'm so so sorry," Alida said, her eyes welling up. "What do you do?"

"I'm a screenwriter."

"Anything I'd know?"

"*Goodbye, October.*"

"No way!" she said, hitting the flat of her hand on the table.

"You've seen it?"

"Sourpuss and I saw it last weekend."

Carissa turned her head and locked into our conversation.

"What did you think?" I asked.

"Are you serious? Freakin' loved it."

Carissa closed one eye and shook her head.

"Tell him the truth," she said.

"Well, I had a little issue with the ending."

"Most people do," I said.

It was true. People took issue with the ending.

"I loved the two characters but thought he would be more empathetic and feel her pain after all he'd been through. Like, I thought all that would have made him stronger, not more closed off."

"So you think he had it in him to help her?"

"I do. But I dunno. Look, it's your film."

"Not really. Once it's out in the world, it belongs to everyone. It comes alive differently for everyone who sees it, you know? I know that and I respect it. That's art."

Alida nodded.

"You see, I fell in love with both of them," she said. "That's why when she walked him out to the car I thought he would have given her the Post-it note."

"That was what I thought too before we worked on it, but once we'd been in the world of the script for a while that felt maybe like the predictable ending, a happy ending."

"So you wanted to make a film just for the surprise."

I looked down at the photo of the dancer, Cory.

"No, I just thought this ending felt more like life."

"Can you be quiet please," a woman from the table behind us whispered.

Alida ignored her.

"But she was the one person who could help him find that truth you kept referring to in your film. And he could have shown her he was getting it if he'd handed her the Post-it. Do you see what I'm saying?"

The lights blinked on and off.

"So why let her go?" I said, placing my reading glasses on the table.

"People need people even if they are made from different cloth. He felt something for her and she for him. She was so willing to just listen and hold him."

The room went black.

"What they had together in those one or two meetings was so deep. I'd never seen a film portray a relationship like that. It was so real."

"So he should have opened up to her and given her the Post-it note? Couldn't the audience understand and feel how real it was even if he didn't go the step of giving her the note?"

"The writing was so good that it still would have given you the surprise ending you wanted, but with a subtle twist."

Cory walked out on stage, and held her position as the music ricocheted off the walls of the tiny theater.

"Thanks for your honesty," I said. "I appreciate it."

"That's why I keep Carissa around."

She rested her hand on Carissa's shoulder.

"Here's my card," I said. "Maybe we can grab a coffee. I'd love to hear what you think about my new film idea."

I looked at my finger and noticed blood trickling down.

"Hey, Izabelle," Tom shouted. "What d'ya think?"

He'd glued bits of colored glass to the door of the car and arranged the potted plants along the ground to highlight and make space for his new mosaic.

"I love it, Tom," Alida called over to him. "You're an artist."

"You still didn't tell me what you thought about on the way over today," Alida said.

A few days after my first encounter with Alida I noticed the large-scale painting that hung in my therapist's office was done by her. She called it, *October Morning*—the name of my film. I thought about that as I walked into the room for my weekly one-hour session. I was feeling better that day and it was having a positive effect on my session. After two years and unspeakable amounts of money and time, I was able to reach down deep and hoist to the surface the guilt I was consumed with following the tragedy. At that moment of revelation, as if a meteor hit me square on the head, my therapist looked at her wrist watch.

I understood that above all this was still a business, but I felt after so much hard work I was owed at least another 10 minutes. My self-realization was that what happened was not because of me, but rather a turn of events that we have no real control over. Like an earthquake causing buildings to topple and mountainsides to crumble, the alignments of people in places at that right or wrong time can seal one's fate, *does* seal fate for people. That admission is what I wanted to say to my doctor. Instead, I watched her turn her wrist as if in slow motion, and stretch her neck to get a good glimpse. Images shot through my head but the one that stuck was of her yawning, slinking horizontal onto the couch and closing her eyes.

"Wake me up when you're finished," she'd say.

I got up, thanked her for her precious time and shut the door behind me. As I walked slowly past the receptionist, I figured maybe my therapist would come out.

"I understand you're angry," she might say and walk me to my car.

But that didn't happen. I told the receptionist I would not pay for the session.

"I'm not paying, and I'm not coming back," I told her, and slipped the paper back toward her.

"I'm not supposed to say this," she said, "but between the two of us, your therapist is the most well respected in the country in dealing with your kind of trauma. It's your prerogative to feel you're being ignored, but maybe, just maybe, her actions were premeditated."

I felt a bit uneasy about her knowledge of what went on beyond the closed doors. My rational self said it was just a coincidence. I wondered if I was not the first to storm out and tell her I was not paying. I wanted this incident with my therapist to be mine. Maybe, I wanted this tragedy and all that came after it to also be just mine. I glanced at the wall where the diplomas from Cornell, Harvard and University of Pennsylvania were displayed, and then settled on Alida's painting with the name of my film, the strangeness of encountering this gesture toward my own work in the office of my own therapist. A mother was holding the hand of a young child. One could only see the back of the woman. She wore a long, sleeveless summer dress. The child had turned to face us. It appeared she was signaling to the viewer with her free hand that something was not right. She squinted as if fearful of the outcome of where they were going. The woman was barefoot with broad shoulders. Her posture was exaggerated as if she was walking on a stage to receive some kind of award. I looked back at the receptionist.

"The only thing premeditated here is the fact I'll not pay for this session."

"I'll mail it to you," she said without expression. "You can take it up with your insurance company."

I walked over to the painting and stared into it.

"You still didn't tell me what you thought about on your way over," Alida called me out from where I'd landed in the past.

After that incident with my therapist, I retreated back into a solitary existence. I came to a decision not to speak about what happened to anyone unless it was a stranger. A guarantee that I'd never see the person again. But the more I shut myself off from the physical world, the more I had to deal with physical pain. I started going to massage therapists. Some of them were legit, and some were well-versed in the art of happy endings. The doctors of happy endings would listen to me up to a point but they wanted to do their thing and get to the next customer.

"How do you want it," they'd ask.

That's when I dressed, paid them for their time and headed out.

Once, or maybe twice, I went to a massage therapist that was different.

"Anything you want?" she said in an accented voice at the beginning of the hour.

I thought about it.

"Would you hold me?"

"Sure, baby. What else?"

"That's it."

I told her the whole story. I felt her arms tighten and then loosen and tighten again around my body. She stayed with me as my therapist had not, and I could feel it. I closed my eyes and told the entire story. When I was done, I opened my eyes and saw her dark brown eyes were filled with tears.

***

"Are you gonna tell me what you were thinking about on the drive over?" says Alida. Her tone has shifted. She sounds concerned.

"Just thinking about a new story for my next film."

Her eyes catch the morning sun.

"I'll get the bandages and rubbing alcohol. Be right back."

Tom is moving the fiddle leaf fig to get it into a new patch of sunlight when suddenly an oversized SUV turns quickly onto the dead-end street and double-parks in front of my spot. Tom's car jerks as the man gets out, slams the heavy door and walks with purpose towards Tom.

"Can you move those plants?"

Tom puts down his watering can and wipes his face with a dirty bandana he pulls from his back pocket.

"It will take me some time to do that."

"You're taking up space here," he says, as he removes his sunglasses. "It's also illegal."

Tom is frozen as if his legs are stuck in cement. A girl in her mid-twenties jumps out of the SUV and runs over to Tom.

"Ignore him. He's an asshole."

"Get the fuck back in the car," the man says.

"You're not my father."

"Get the fuck in the car."

Alida pushes open the old warehouse door holding a first-aid kit. She steps off the platform of the building and walks quickly over to the girl.

"You OK?"

"Get the fuck away from her," the man says, grabbing the fiddle leaf fig tree and throwing it on the pile of plastic tubes where Tom had thrown what was left in the box a few minutes before.

"Now I have room to park."

Alida positions her body between him and the girl.

"He's allowed to be here," she says. "You have no right to throw his plant."

"Get the fuck back in the car," he yells to the girl.

"I'm done," she says, throwing a wad of crumpled cash at his face. "I don't need your money."

"Pick it up."

She turns her body toward the platform and locks in on my eyes. I look over at the fiddle leaf fig tree lying like a corpse on the pile of broken plastic tubes. I remember my daughter told me that before she went on her trip she gave her own giant fiddle leaf fig tree away to a friend. It broke her heart as she had nurtured it in her tiny studio apartment in Brooklyn when she moved there after college. I recall she told me the mild-mannered fiddle leaf fig in the wild can actually be a bit of a bully toward other plants in its native community. She said they have a peculiar way of getting ahead in life by dropping their seeds and lodging in crevices of the roots of taller host plants. As they grow, the young fig plant sends down long, sturdy roots straight into the ground. And as more roots come down they surround, overwhelm, and eventually kill the host tree and the new tree will stand alone on the new structure it's built.

"I said get the fuck back in the car, bitch."

As the girl ascends the concrete slabs, I notice a tattoo on her arm. It is familiar but I can't remember where I've seen it before. Her floral mini dress is slightly soiled with blood and her eye makeup is smudged and running down her cheeks. I shade my eyes from the sun and am reminded of the painting I purchased from Alida that hangs in my house. I remember the face of my daughter the last time I saw her. Like muscle memory that returns when you get on a bicycle for the first time in years, I open my arms as she gets closer. At that moment the ending of my next film comes into light. Looking out at the chaotic scene unfolding down below I put pieces together and see an opening for the redemption of the failed ending of October Morning. I can see now that Alida was right. Izabelle. By any name, she was right. The ending had been a missed opportunity, a failure. I'd shied in a crucial moment away from something important. As if in slow motion, the girl, Izabelle, presses against my body, and I hold on to her.

***

I look down at my new name printed across the title page of the final draft of The Ending and wonder. I read it again and feel a new sense of freedom. I think of those Buddhist monks who strip off every material thing to get somewhere new.

"Anonymity," she whispers, pressing her hand gently on my shoulder. "Where's your toolkit?"

I point to the cabinet underneath the kitchen sink.

"I like that song on your playlist."

"Which one?"

"The one about questioning God," she says. "Couple words I don't understand, but…"

"That's a great song. It's Leonard Cohen. I'll play it again."

I hear the sound of light tapping coming from the living room.

"Take a break for a minute and come look at what I did," she says.

My brain quickly organizes the patterns and makes sense of the shapes of the large painting now occupying my wall space.

"I took down the old one."

"You didn't like it?"

"I didn't think it paired well with this one. Like two different stories. Do you see what I mean?"

Turning my head, I stare at the figure holding the hammer and connect her with the new painting.

"I stuck the Post-it note in the woman's hand like Izabelle said."

I remembered crossing the bridge on that day when my thoughts went to the water below. How it must feel when your car lands and then begins to sink and the electric windows don't respond when you try to get them to open, when you are trying to survive this. An ending that I'd prefer but felt the viewer wouldn't be able to stomach the correlation between fiction and my truth. How could they?

Like dance partners locked in choreography, we both step back from the large painting. I glance at the full-length mirror as the music plays inside me. At the moment the photons settle in my brain, a warm breeze blows through the open window and envelops my body like a warm blanket. When the reflection in the mirror finally clarifies, I run my hand over my freshly-shaved head. The skin is smooth and nick-free. Everything that was is now lost in the past. But now there's more. I can feel it expanding in front of me, and I marvel that I needed to get to the end to see over the edge.

"Not sure it's needed anymore," I say, and step slowly toward the figure now occupying my space. I step toward her and hold out my arms.

Paul Rabinowitz is a writer, photographer and founder of ARTS By The People, a non-profit arts organization. He is the author of 6 books. Rabinowitz's photography, prose and poetry appear in magazines and journals including *The Sun Magazine, New World Writing, Arcturus-Chicago Review Of Books, Evening Street Press, The Montreal Review, Stone Poetry Quarterly, Talking River Review*, and elsewhere. Rabinowitz was a featured artist in *Nailed Magazine* in 2020, *Mud Season Review* in 2022, *Apricity Press* in 2023, *Rappahannock Review* in 2024 and *The Woven Tale Press* in 2025. His photo series Limited Light was nominated for Best of the Net in 2021. Rabinowitz's poems and fiction are the inspiration for 8 award winning experimental films, including Best Experimental Short at Cannes, Venice Independent Film Festival, and others.

www.paulrabinowitz.com

www.ingramcontent.com/pod-product-compliance
Lightning Source LLC
Chambersburg PA
CBHW031225170426
43191CB00031B/522